Harriet Warner Ellis

Denmark and Her Missions

Dedicated by permission to Her Majesty the Queen Dowager of Denmark

Harriet Warner Ellis

Denmark and Her Missions
Dedicated by permission to Her Majesty the Queen Dowager of Denmark

ISBN/EAN: 9783337324926

Printed in Europe, USA, Canada, Australia, Japan

Cover: Foto ©ninafisch / pixelio.de

More available books at **www.hansebooks.com**

DENMARK AND HER MISSIONS.

HER MAJESTY THE QUEEN OF DENMARK.

HARRI...
AUTHOR OF "TOILS A...

SEELEY, JACKSON, AND HALLIDAY, 54 FLEET STREET.
LONDON. MDCCCLXII.

TO

Her Majesty the Queen Dowager of Denmark,

THE PATRON AND PROMOTER

OF BIBLE AND MISSIONARY EFFORTS,

THIS LITTLE VOLUME

IS,

BY HER ROYAL PERMISSION,

MOST RESPECTFULLY DEDICATED

BY

HER MAJESTY'S OBEDIENT HUMBLE SERVANT

THE AUTHOR.

CONTENTS.

		Page.
I.—INTRODUCTION.		1
II.—CHRONICLES OF THE PAST		5
III.—DENMARK AS IT IS		16
IV.—MATRIMONIAL ALLIANCES		30
V.—INDIA		41
VI.—FIRST DANISH MISSIONARIES		58
VII.—HELP FROM ENGLAND		76
VIII.—TRANQUEBAR		95
IX.—SWARTZ		110
X.—VISIT TO TANJORE		123
XI.—CAREY		130
XII.—SERAMPORE		139
XIII.—BOMBAY AND THE DANISH SEAMAN		160
XIV.—GREENLAND		167
XV.—MATTHEW AND CHRISTIAN STACH		179
XVI.—JOYS AND SORROWS		191
XVII.—WEST INDIAN ISLANDS		210
XVIII.—ST. JAN		227
XIX.—THE TRANSLATED BIBLE AND ITS FRIENDS		242
XX.—CONCLUSION		258

Denmark and her Missions.

CHAPTER. I.

INTRODUCTION.

" Whether Saxon or Dane, or Norman we,
   Teuton, or Celt, or whatever we be,
   We are each *all Dane* in our welcome to thee,
—Tennyson.   Alexandra!"

THE recent marriage of the Princess Alexandra with His Royal Highness the Prince of Wales, excited throughout the whole of the British empire, the deepest interest about Denmark, and everything connected with that country. The words quoted from our Laureate do not in any degree exaggerate the loyal and affectionate welcome with which Her Royal Highness was greeted.

As the result, information about herself and her family, and the country of her father's adoption, is eagerly sought, and already are Danish professors engaged in teaching willing pupils its language. The father of the Princess of Wales is not by birth a member of the Danish royal family, but belongs to the House of Glucksburg. The Princess Louisa, his wife, is of the House of Hesse Cassel. The Princess Alexandra is one of a family of six, having two sisters, the Princesses Dagmar and Thyra; and three brothers, the second of whom has just been elected King of Greece, under the title of George I. In endeavouring to obtain information about Denmark, the author has unexpectedly found, that in addition to those attractions, with which recent events, and the former connexion between that country and England invested the subject, Denmark has a still higher claim to the interest and gratitude of the whole Protestant world.

A King of Denmark first originated and supported Protestant missions to the Heathen.

The chief object of this little book is to trace the history and progress of these missions. While the writer is fully sensible that it can lay claim to no literary merit, she trusts that the accounts compiled from so many reliable sources will not be without interest to the Christian reader. In narrating facts, she feels she is treading upon solid ground.

If the interest of Christians at home in the conversion of the Heathen is to be excited and maintained, it is of the utmost importance, that truthful accounts should be given of mission life.

Little of the literature of Denmark is open to those who are uninitiated in its language, as but few of its standard works have been translated into English. From the somewhat scanty materials available in English and German, the subsequent details have been gleaned.

The facts are to be found in the following authorities:—Crantz's History of the Greenland Mission; Ollendorp's History; Egede's History and Life; Brown's History of Missions; History and Periodicals of the United Brethren; Mosheim's Ecclesiastical History; Robertson's History of the Christian Church; Danish Conferences; Dr. Pearson's Life of Buchanan; Christian Researches by Dr. Buchanan; Denmark and the Duchies, by Lang; Marryat's Jutland; Life and Times of Carey, Marshman and Ward; Swartz's Life; Bishop Holmes's Historical Sketches, and several scarce old books, to be found only in the British Museum.

The writer subsequently obtained the invaluable works of the Rev. James Hough, from which many extracts are made. She is also much indebted to the Rev. W. F. Bullock, Secretary to the Society for the Propagation of the Gospel in Foreign Parts, for the kindness and courtesy with which he placed the reports, and other volumes elucidating the early history of the Tranquebar Mission, at her disposal. The late much esteemed Rev. Peter La Trobe, whose lamented death took place while these pages were passing through the press, was one, to whom the writer had tendered her warm thanks.

He most kindly furnished her with much valuable information respecting the Greenland Missions, and it will ever be a melancholy satisfaction to recall the fact, that one of the last of his many acts of kindness was, to revise the chapters in this book, relating to that Mission.

A brief sketch of the Royal House of Denmark, and of the past matrimonial connexions between that country and England has also been introduced.

If this little volume should but deepen interest in the cause of missions, and sympathy with the heroic men engaged in the work; still more, if it should induce one faithful Christian to devote himself to this glorious undertaking, the end of the writer would be abundantly answered.

CHAPTER II.

CHRONICLES OF THE PAST.

> "Denmark, whose roving hordes in barbarous times
> Filled the wide world with piracy and crimes;
> Awed every shore, and taught their keels to sweep
> O'er every sea, the Arabs of the deep."

THE first connected account which we have of Denmark, is to be found in the work of Jornandes, called "De Rebus Gothicis."

From it we learn, that the ancient inhabitants of that country were remarkable for their bravery. Tacitus, who wrote of them as early as A.D. 98, speaks of the Danes as a body "small in number, but great in renown;" and mentions the large encampments of brave soldiers, which then existed on both sides of their Chersonesus, as a proof of the strength and power of the nation. Plutarch tells us, that 300,000 Danes made an excursion at one time into Italy.

Many fables, which grave historians have called facts, may be found scattered through the history of this country. An ancient archbishop of Upsal solemnly assures us, that, after the flood, Noah became king of the whole earth: and that his grandson, Magog, son of Japhet, was the first King of Denmark. Dunham, in his history of Northern Europe, tells us, that Harold was the first king who openly professed the so-called new religion, on account of which his name is held very dear. "Although," he says, "Christianity had been introduced long before the reign of Canute, it was not till his time that it began to impart those personal and social effects with which it is fraught."

At an early period in the ninth century, a Christian mission to Jutland was undertaken by two ecclesiastics, named Ansgar and Authbert; the former a monk of Westphalia, the latter a Frenchman.

A petty king of Jutland, named Herald Klack, being driven from his throne, implored the aid of Louis Charlemagne against the usurper. His request was granted, on condition that he would embrace Christianity, and admit the ministers of religion to preach in his dominions. For the two following years, these laborious missionaries went through Jutland and Cimbria, declaring the Gospel of Christ. So great was the opposition excited, that no persuasions could induce any one to accompany them in the capacity of a servant, and they had to perform the most menial offices for themselves.

On one of their voyages the vessel in which Ansgar sailed, encountered some pirates, who captured the ship, and robbed the venerable man of the whole of his property. Amongst the things whose loss he the most deplored, were forty volumes of manuscript, some of them books of Holy Scripture, which he had collected with much labour, for the use of the mission.

After preaching the Gospel in Jutland, Ansgar, joined by a clergyman named Vitman, resolved to visit Sweden. They encountered many hardships during a long and wearisome journey, before they arrived at the capital. It was then called Birca, and is the site of modern Stockholm. Here they were most graciously received by the king. He gave them permission to preach to his subjects, and they soon witnessed most happy results from their labours.

Returning to Germany, Ansgar was loaded with honours by Louis the Meek; and was created Archbishop of Hamburgh and the North of Europe. In the performance of his clerical duties, he frequently travelled amongst the Danes, to promote the cause of Christ, to form new churches, and to establish those which were already gathered. The permission now granted by the king for freedom of religious worship in Denmark, induced many Danish traders, who had received baptism at Hamburg and elsewhere, now openly to profess Christianity in their own country. Merchants from distant parts began to traffic more frequently with Denmark, so that the Danish monarch found the wealth of his kingdom increased by the toleration he had granted.

This was followed by a time of persecution. After the death of the old king, Hovi, Earl of Jutland, persuaded Eric II. that his misfortunes in war were owing to his abandonment of idolatry. The church at Schleswig was shut up, and the Christians were cruelly treated. Ere long, Hovi himself fell into disgrace, and was banished. Then Ansgar received a letter from the young king, urging his return, and professing a warm interest in the Gospel. The progress of Christianity was now more rapid than ever. A second church was founded at Ripe, and Rembert, a convert, was appointed its pastor. Ansgar continued his glorious course till his death in 865. This good work was confined to the mainland. The islands continued altogether Pagan, till permission was obtained from the king that Christians should be allowed freedom of religious service in them also, and that human sacrifices should cease. "We have thus seen," says Mosheim, "that some scattered rays of divine light had penetrated into Denmark." The effects of the Gospel in that country were so apparent in the twelfth century that the historian, Adam of Bremen, writes thus concerning it, " Look at that ferocious nation of the Danes. For a long time they have now been accustomed to sing the praises of God! Survey that piratical people; now they are contented with the productions of their own country. Contemplate that horrid region, formerly inaccessible on account of idolatry, now they cordially admit the preachers of the truth."

Having thus briefly alluded to the introduction of Christianity into Denmark, we will take a rapid glance at some points of interest in the country itself.

While there is much in Denmark to surprise and amuse a British traveller, there is also much to remind him of his own land. Almost every city and fort has some legend attached to it. One of their chroniclers tells how, in a coasting expedition, he stopped near Denmark's Lilya, better known as Danaholm, once the boundary line of the three northern kingdoms, a sort of neutral ground, where in 951 the kings of these three countries met. After enjoying much pleasant intercourse, the table was laid, and the cloth spread for a royal repast, when the three sovereigns dined together, each one sitting in his own dominions. The chronicler ends with telling us, that when the hour for parting arrived, the King of Norway held the stirrup, and the King of Denmark the reins, while the King of Sweden mounted his horse. No doubt the worthy chronicler was himself a Swede!

Many of the public buildings have historical associations connecting them with both countries. This is the case in the town of Sonderborg, whose fine old castle stands out by the water-side. It is sadly dilapidated now, and bereft of all its fine towers save one. It was once a very strong fortress, the residence of the Dukes of Schleswig. In the chapel stands erect the armour of Duke John, son of King Christian III. Here, and elsewhere, the traveller is reminded of the unhappy Bothwell, and many stirring events connected with Denmark and Scotland are said to have taken place within these grim old fortresses. The national ballads contain sundry amusing rhymes about King Valdemar and his young Queen Dagmar, who died in the castle of Skanderborg. In it Queen Anne, consort of James I., first saw the light. This castle possesses an additional interest from its having been, during his early days, the residence of the Crown Prince Frederick, afterwards Frederick VI. This monarch, following in the steps of his predecessors, proved a warm and liberal friend and patron to the cause of Christian missions. In the library of Copenhagen there may still be seen a copy of the Book of Proverbs, presented to Prince Frederick's tutor, by the king. Within, is the following inscription, in the king's own hand, "I gave this book to Master Hans, my son's chastiser, here in Skanderborg." More legends are told of this king than of any other member of the Royal House.

When James I. visited Copenhagen, he made a special pilgrimage to the city of Roeskilda, anciently Rothschild, in order to converse on theology with Nicholas Hemming, a divine who, on account of his Calvinistic tendencies, had been removed from his Professorship in the University of Copenhagen.

As a proof of the similarity of names and languages, between the two nations, it is not uncommon to say of a Jutlander, "He speaks very bad Danish, it is so like English." Marryat, in his "Jutland," gives an interesting corroboration of this fact. "During his residence in Copenhagen," he says, "We were talking over English names, of which so many are to be met with in Denmark, when a lady, who devotes herself to teaching in the poor schools of this city, told us of the intense interest taken by the school-children during the Indian war, in the fortunes of Sir Henry Havelock, our British General. The morning the news of his death arrived, she found the whole of her school dissolved in tears, weeping their very hearts out, for they looked upon him as their own countryman, the very 'Havelock the Dane' of the popular ballad, the lapse of nine or ten centuries being nothing to their infant minds."

Sir Henry was perhaps more grieved over by the children of Denmark, from this early nursery association, than even by those in the British Empire. The story of Havelock is related by the earliest French poet known, Geoffroi Ganier, 1147, and is styled, "Le Lai d' Avalok." It is shortly this, "Ethelwuld, King of England, had an only daughter, whom, at his death, he confided to the care of Godrich, Earl of Cornwall. The Princess Guldborg was very beautiful, and when she attained the age of twenty, the time for her to succeed to the kingdom of her father, the false Earl determined to make his own son king instead. At the same period, the King of Denmark died under similar circumstances, and bequeathed his children, Prince Havelock, and his two sisters, to the protection of Godard, who, the story says, was as great a traitor as was ever known, next to Judas. He immured the children in a prison for three years, where they suffered both from cold and hunger. At last he put the daughters to death, and Havelock would have shared the same fate had he not renounced all claim to the Crown of

Denmark. But Godard soon repented his clemency, and gave Havelock to his servant Grim to drown. He carried the Prince home to his hut, tied up in a sack, to be thrown at night into the sea. But a wonderful light over the boy frightened Grim and his wife, and they determined to save the son of their king. They fled from Denmark, taking Havelock with them. The wind carried the vessel to England, where they landed at the entrance of the Humber. Here they built a house, and lived by fishing. The place was called Grimsby, and it is a curious fact, that the town of Grimsby, founded by the Dane Grim, enjoyed for many years an exemption from payment of the sound-duties at Elsinore. Havelock helped Grim in his fishing, but in a year of scarcity he went to Lincoln, where he was employed by Earl Godrich's cook. When the Earl saw Havelock, he determined to marry him to the Princess Guldborg, and thus fulfil the promise he had given to her father, to get for her the strongest and handsomest man in England. Fearing treachery, after the marriage Havelock and his bride left Lincoln for Grimsby. Grim was dead; so Havelock, accompanied by Grim's five sons, returned to Denmark, where he was recognized by Ubbe, who declaring in his favour, Havelock was proclaimed King of Denmark. He returned to England, conquered Earl Godrich in a battle at Grimsby, and was then proclaimed King of England. King Havelock rewarded all those who had shown him kindness. Grim's daughter, Gunhild, he married to the Earl of Chester. The cook, his old master, he created Earl of Cornwall, and Ubbo became Stadtholder of Denmark.

In corroboration of this identity of names, it is interesting to observe that all our English cinque ports have names of Scandinavian origin.

Near the ancient fort of Skanderborg, of which mention has been already made, there is the ruin of the old church of *Dover*. Further on to the left lies *Rye*. *Sandwig*, formerly spelt *Sandwich*, lies by the sea-coast. *Hastings* derives her title from the pirate chief; and *Winchelsea*, from another called Vinkels.

There is certainly no romance in the names of some of the Jutland nobility, but we meet with their counterparts in our own land. Names derived from the swine tribe seem in vogue there, as Boar, Hog, Pig. Oxe, Kalf, and Krabbe are also not uncommon.

Amongst the inhabitants of the East of England many still retain names, now common in Denmark. The Rothschild family were among those who emigrated from that country. There are many towns and villages along the east coast of Yorkshire and Lincolnshire still bearing Danish names; as Thurtelby, Spilsby, Grimsby, Rigsby. The termination *by* generally indicates a Danish origin.

CHAPTER III.

DENMARK AS IT IS.

"Let thine eye look like a friend upon Denmark."
SHAKESPEARE.

WE have already seen that the connexion between England and Denmark is of long standing. It began in 787, in war and bloodshed. Its last incident has been the joyous union of the heir apparent of England's crown, with the lovely scion of the Royal House of Denmark.

The interval has been filled up, so far as our own country is concerned, with events, the traditions of which are familiar to every reader of English history. Much of uncertainty must however prevail as to the accuracy of the early details.

For these we are dependent upon the venerable Bede. He had only oral tradition to rely upon, and three hundred years elapsed between the events themselves and the time when he committed them to writing.

The main facts are, that the Danes did invade England, and that they obtained a permanent footing under Sweyn in 1012.

The Danes were divided into three tribes called the Juti, Angli, and Frisi. They preserved in England, as they do still in their fatherland, their distinct languages and usages; and during their abode in our island they frequently made war upon each other.

Canute, the greatest of their princes, assumed the title of King of England, Norway, Denmark, and Sweden. On the death of his son Hardicanute, in 1041, the line of Danish monarchs in England ended.

"The similarity of character and spirit in the Danes and English," writes Mr. Laing, in his interesting book called "Denmark and the Duchies," "has produced a remarkable similarity of social and political results from institutions and forms of government, established on the most opposite theoretical principles. Like plants from the same stock, which produce the same flowers and fruit, under the most different circumstances of soil, climate, or culture, the Dane and the Englishman retain, under the most opposite forms of government, the same attachment to the civil liberty of the individual, the same veneration for their old institutions, the same love of country, the same loyalty, and the same common sense and practical kind of mind and character in private and public affairs. No two European nations with different languages, laws, institutions, and governments, and with so little intercourse with each other, are so alike in character, spirit, way of thinking and acting, as the Danish and the English." It was in 1660, as most readers of modern history know, that the Government of Denmark was, by a solemn act of the States, vested absolutely in the king; and yet, strange to say, the people enjoy an amount of liberty wholly unknown under many liberal Governments. Mr. Laing says,—" If Diogenes had lived in our times, he might have laughed or railed at the inconsistencies of modern nations, to see the most constitutional Government in Europe—that which other nations desire to imitate, but want the materials to do so—that in which civil, political, and religious liberty, freedom of the press, trial by jury, and a representation of the people in the Legislature, are realities, standing very far behind the most autocratical Government in Europe—that in which the kingly power was made absolute and supreme by a solemn act of the nation,—in very many of those landmarks, by which the comparative progress of nations in civilization and moral and intellectual culture is measured, in the administration of law, and the abolition of imprisonment for debt beyond a fixed period, in the education of the people, in the advancement of Christianity abroad, in the encouragement of science, literature, and the fine arts at home. The code of laws drawn up by the Chancellor Griffenfeld, himself a man of the people, the son of a wine merchant, is so clear, simple, and concise, being all contained in one small volume—is so impartial and liberal withal, in the equal protection of property and liberty to all classes, that Norway retains to this day, with the most democratic constitution of government in Europe, the same laws for the protection of person and property that she lived under when a province of the absolute monarchy of Denmark. The cabinet councillors, or ministers, yield, as with us, to the force of public opinion on public affairs, and adopt or renounce measures, and retire or retain place, with the same sensitive regard to their own consistency of principle and character in their political conduct. Public opinion is expressed as clearly and effectively as in England. The social polity of Denmark and England has been as different as their political economy. The social philosopher might well ask how two nations could arrive at nearly the same state of wellbeing and civilization by roads so entirely opposite?" The Danish Government was the first in Europe which furnished the means of education to the people, establishing school-houses in every

2*

parish, and salaries for every teacher. In his amusing book on Jutland, Marryat says,—" If good Lord Shaftesbury imagines, because he has established ragged schools in England by his philanthropy, that he invented them, he is mistaken; for here a similar institution for poor houseless vagabonds existed in the middle ages." Denmark also opened normal schools for teaching schoolmasters long before England established them. But here it wisely stopped. It did not, like the Prussian and other German Governments, attempt to *force* education upon the lower orders—to take the training of the children out of the hands of their parents, and compel their attendance at National Schools, without reference to the wishes, social position, or requirements of their family. In Denmark, parents are free to educate their children as they please, and any one is free to keep a school. "Men from the middle and lower classes have raised themselves by their talents to the highest positions in the State in Denmark as frequently as in England, since the revolutions in the two countries of 1660 and 1688; but the constitutional Governments stand behind the despotic in throwing aside all class favouritism or family influence, and appointing the most able, without regard to birth, fortune, or party, to the highest State offices. The confidence reposed by the public authorities in the good behaviour of the people is very striking. The seats, and monuments, and trees, and shrubs, in the parks, and public walks, require no protection but the good feeling of the public; there is very little drunkenness; the people seem all to have a home of some kind, and the houseless, as a class, are unknown. The population increases but slowly. The inhabitants are principally engaged in agriculture, there being little manufacture except for home use. Having neither metals nor minerals, the country possesses no capabilities for supplying foreign consumers."* Denmark has no harbours on the North Sea, her navigation being confined to the Baltic. There is no ebb and flow of the waters on the eastern shore of this peninsula. This fact may have given rise to the tale about Canute, with which we are edified in all the popular Histories of England. It is probable that the origin of this traditionary anecdote may have been the curiosity of the Danes, who had never seen the phenomenon of flood and ebb in the Baltic, and would naturally point it out to the king, and desire him to control it.

In 1397, Denmark, Norway, and Sweden were united under one crown, by the Treaty of Calmar. Sweden renounced the union in 1523, but the

---

* "Denmark and the Duchies," pp. 286 and 394.

other two kingdoms remained connected down to 1814, when Norway was annexed to Sweden. The Danes proper, or inhabitants of Jutland and the islands, belong to the Scandinavian branch of the Teutonic family; the inhabitants of the Duchies, to the German branch.

Into the vexed question relating to the recent hostilities between the two races, it is no part of our business to enter. One of the papers of the day says:—" The Danish political horizon looks brighter than it has done for some time. The result of the late meeting of kings is looked for with great interest, as it can hardly mean less than an earnest attempt on the part of Sweden to meet Denmark half way, and thus overcome all hindrances to a united policy.

"The national spirit of Denmark has always been kept up by the memory of her former greatness. The recent meeting between Charles XV. and Frederick VIII. may be followed by important results. This is earnestly to be desired, not only for their own sakes, but for the sake of Europe. It may ultimately again lead to a powerful and united Scandinavia."

Reference has already been made to the singular union of absolute power and paternal government in the reigning sovereign. A curious instance is mentioned by a recent writer. An

Englishman, who had brought a menagerie of wild animals to the capital, was in the habit of putting his head into the mouth of the lion. The police interfered to prevent an act fraught with danger to life; but the proprietor, who made money by the exhibition, complained to the British Minister. The only answer he could obtain was, that in Denmark, human life must not be exposed to such a risk. The king's regard for the security of his subjects' personal property is manifest by another law, which prevents foreigners from obtaining the necessary signature to their passports, until they produce a statement from the landlord of their hotel certifying that they are not in debt.

The city of Copenhagen itself is full of objects of interest. In addition to the Royal galleries of pictures by the best masters, there is a public library, containing more than 150,000 volumes, besides many rare books and manuscripts.

The Rev. C. B. Elliott, in his "Letters from the North of Europe," mentions, as an object of special interest, the Crown Battery. It is erected on an island formed by ships sunk, with huge stones regularly ranged on them. It is constructed on the same principle as the breakwater at Plymouth. He says,—"As we sailed over the spot where, in 1801, Nelson fought the battle that decided the right of England to search foreign ships, and as we saw the Three-Crown Battery, that poured its heavy artillery on our vessels, I could not but feel that local circumstances rendered more than probable the Danish story, that two of his vessels had been destroyed by their guns, and were actually stranded at the time that Nelson sent to know if they would comply with England's terms. If this be the fact, the *battle* was *theirs*, the *success ours*." The death of the brave Danes who fell on that occasion is commemorated by the following motto on a monument erected by the king:—

"They *fell*, but Denmark *stood*."

In the Museum there is a MS. of the Apocalypse of St. John, in Latin, beautifully executed and ornamented with pictures. It is supposed to have been written in the tenth century.

Copenhagen is really a picturesque city, with its canals alive with shipping. It contains a large number of palaces and public buildings, though, like all fortified towns, it boasts of no handsome entrance.

The Castle of Rosenburg is, perhaps, the most interesting of the public edifices. The architecture is Gothic. It contains a silver throne, and two enormous candlesticks, eight feet in height a vase used at the Royal christenings, and other antiques in the same precious metal. It is no longer a Royal habitation, though formerly the sovereigns used to resort to it in the spring; and it was here Christian IV. died. The cemetery of the Danish capital is a miniature of that of Père la Chaise, in Paris. One of the four smaller palaces, is now occupied by the present Queen Dowager, the universally beloved widow of King Christian VIII., and a second by the Landgrave of Hesse, brother to the Duchess of Cambridge.

Besides Copenhagen, there are many Danish cities of great interest; amongst them is Viborg, on a hill overlooking a lake of the same name, where in ancient times sovereigns were elected for the provinces of Jutland, and where in Pagan days were solemnized the chief sacrifices to the god Odin. Many historical events of great import are connected with this old city; and in later days it is interesting as the birth-place of Hans Tausen, the Luther of Denmark.

In the sixteenth century, when all Europe was filled with rumours of the Wittemberg monk, there rose up a grey brother, who, in defiance of all priestly authority, preached the doctrines of the Reformation in Denmark, and Viborg became the first Protestant city in the kingdom. The national religion in Denmark is Lutheran.

The old round tower churches in several of the islands are very striking to the eye of a stranger. Small turret staircases lead to the upper stories, through the loopholes of which archers and men-at-arms shot forth their arrows. In one of them may yet be seen suspended from the pulpit four hour-glasses. They were presented when clocks were not in general use, and at a time when the early Lutheran clergy indulged in very long sermons. These discourses were afterwards limited to one hour, and hour-glasses were fixed by the side of each pulpit. It is added by the author, on whose authority these facts are stated, that in order to maintain even-handed justice between the preacher and his hearers, as the former were not allowed to exceed one hour in their sermons, that 'Kirke-Gubber,' or church-pushers, were appointed in 1688, whose duty it was to arouse any lethargic hearers, and to prevent them from indulging in sleep during the time of divine service, and that for this duty they received an annual stipend of six dollars.

Amongst the events of the deepest interest in the history of Denmark is the fact, that to that country must be awarded the honour of being the first of the European Powers which proscribed the infamous traffic of the slave trade.

One of the peculiarities connected with the

physical condition of Denmark is the entire absence of all mountains. Its highest hills rise only about 1,200 feet above the sea. Towards the west, where the Jutland Peninsula terminates in the Baltic, the country is so barren and desolate, that it has been compared by some writers to Arabia, only that it does not possess its rivers or its verdant oases. Its sands, like those in the East, often overwhelm the feeble agriculture, at which the inhabitants have long been toiling; and when that event occurs, it converts the penury of the Jutlanders into absolute want.

The great extent of seaboard gives Denmark a character which distinguishes it from every other country in Europe. The coast is indented by numerous firths, called fiords, affording many advantages in a commercial point of view. The Sound, which connects Helsingoer and Helsingborg, is considered to be the most frequented strait in the whole world. The air is more humid and damp than that of other countries in the same latitude, owing to the extent of coast; and thick fogs are very frequent. The cold is so severe in winter as frequently to prevent the navigation of the neighbouring seas, through the prevalence of ice. The summer, which lasts from June to September, is often intensely hot.

The Universities are at Copenhagen and Kiel.

The young nobility are educated at Scröa. There is also a number of high schools in the kingdom.

The literature of Ancient Scandinavia may be traced back to remote antiquity. It is of extreme interest to Germany and England. Both of these countries having been Christianised at a very early period, possess no other literary relics of their Pagan ancestors than those which have been preserved in the extreme north. Modern Denmark has produced scholars whose names would confer honour on any nation. The learned Danes speak elegant Latin; while German, English, and French, are very generally understood.

There are eighty periodical works published in Denmark.

We conclude this sketch of Denmark with the following interesting statistics from "The Times," October 2nd, 1863:—"From the last census in Denmark, we find that the whole Danish monarchy has a population somewhat above $2\frac{3}{4}$ millions, of which about 2,600,000 live in Denmark proper, Schleswig, Holstein and Lauenburg, and 150,000 in the Danish Colonies out of Europe.

"The increase of the population during the five years preceding the census was between five and six per cent. Copenhagen numbers 155,000 inhabitants; next, Altona, 45,000. Kiel and Flensburg, between 15,000 and 20,000. Odense,

Schleswig, Aarhuus, Rendsburg and Aalborg, between 5,000 and 10,000 inhabitants. The average population on a Danish square mile (about eighteen English) is 2,532. The Islands and Holstein are better populated than Jutland and Schleswig. Out of an average of 1,000 inhabitants, 241 live in towns; 395 live by agriculture; 228 by trades and manufactures; 187 are labourers; fifty-three commercial men; twenty-nine mariners, twenty paupers, sixteen ministers or schoolmasters, fifteen pensioners, thirteen servants, nine officers in the army and navy, nine capitalists, seven following literary pursuits, including students, five have no fixed modes of living, and a little over one are 'kept locked up by their country, for their country's good.'"

CHAPTER IV.

MATRIMONIAL ALLIANCES.

"Draw back the dusky curtain of the past,
  And cast a retrospective glance with me."

LET us now take a glance at the matrimonial ties, which have united England with Denmark in past times. The late events having awakened sympathy with everything Danish, we, as Britons, are startled, and in some cases almost ashamed, to find how little we know of Denmark and her people.

In reviewing our past relations with that country, there are many points of interest, and though all have not been of the most amicable kind, there are some which doubtless were productive of benefits to both nations. We will not inflict upon our readers the long pedigree of Danish kings, which is said to be traced back as far as to Helge, the Heathen conqueror of Jutland.

About 1,000 years ago, Gorm, an ancient Danish king, of whom little is recorded, became enamoured of the fair Princess Thyra, daughter of Ethelred, King of England, after whom no doubt the sister of the Princess of Wales is named.

An old chronicle tells us that this princess was ambitious as well as fair, and that she refused to become Queen of East Anglia and Denmark, unless Jutland and the adjoining islands were made over to her as a marriage portion.

There is no doubt that this union of races was very advantageous to the Celtic inhabitants of Britain. It may have tended greatly to develop that maritime taste, which leads us proudly to speak of our country as Queen of the Ocean.

In the legends of Denmark, allusion is often made to another of England's daughters, whose memory seems fondly cherished by her northern relatives, Philippa, the sister of the victor of Agincourt.

The history of those times recounts the splendid embassy which arrived from Denmark to escort "Dame Philippa over the sea." As a contrast to the present facility of intercourse it is amusing to quote the words of the chronicler. He says,— "On the 11th of August, 1405, the last farewells were taken, and melancholy they must have been, for the remoteness of the region that was to be Philippa's home, would preclude any feasible hope of future intercourse. On reaching Helsingborg she was met and welcomed by Queen Margaret, and her future lord, and thence conducted to Lund, then the capital of Sweden, where she was married with regal magnificence; and then crowned Queen of Denmark, Norway, and Sweden; and, when the feast and marriage was done, the lords and ladies took their leave and came home again to England; thanked be God in all his doings." A Danish writer says,—" England gave Eric a wife who, by her wise counsels, transfers on herself the whole care of these kingdoms. She rules the people by her virtues. She is a new guardian angel."

She seems to have imbibed much of the martial spirit of her brother: for we are told that, in an attack made on Copenhagen, in 1428, she defended that city with great valour. Her naval efforts did not prove equally successful, for, venturing out to sea, she was repulsed by the inhabitants of Hamburg and Lubeck, and had great difficulty in making her way back to Copenhagen. Her cruel husband, King Eric, resented her defeat, and treated her with such indignity on her return, that she retired to a convent, where she soon after died.

After a lapse of years another Anglo-Danish marriage took place. The historian tells us that King Christian IV. was so anxious to secure an English maiden as his bride, that he sent to Queen Elizabeth an envoy telling her of his wish, and begging her aid and advice. But our maiden

Queen was no friend to matrimony, and does not seem to have vouchsafed any response to these friendly overtures. A few years later, Christian, having solaced himself with a Danish bride, gave his consent to the union of his sister Anne with James VI. of Scotland, who, in due time, came to be King of England.

The memoirs of Sir James Melville, the statesman historian of Scotland, afford much interesting information respecting this alliance. Anne was the second daughter of Frederick II., King of Denmark and Norway, by Sophia of Mecklenburg, a princess who stood high in general esteem for her many domestic virtues. "She is," wrote a spy whom Burleigh had employed to report the characters of the Danish royal family, "a right virtuous and godly princess, who, with a motherly care and great wisdom, ruleth her children." When the little princess was about ten years old, Sir J. Melville tells us, there were divers negotiations on foot for the restoration of the Orkney and Shetland Islands. Nearly a century before, James III. of Scotland had married a princess of Denmark, and her brother, King Christian I., had, in an emergency, pawned those islands to his Scottish brother-in-law. The latter soon found the wonderful advantage which arose from his new possessions, which had long been a sort of rendezvous for the piratical sea kings.

For some years the sovereignty of these islands was a subject of debate, when a courtier suggested that the difficulty might be brought to a happy issue by a marriage between the royal families of Scotland and Denmark. The Scottish king was in no little perplexity when Frederick's ambassadors arrived at Dunfermline. The quaint old chronicler, who wrote his "Historie of King James the Sext," says,—"James was so brave a prince that the noble King Frederick II. of Denmark, having twa doghters, was willing, suld it please our king, to give him the choice of thaim, or that he wauld accept the ane as suld be the maist comely." But though a king, James was by no means his own master. There were already two other fair maidens pointed out as suitable consorts; and while James would fain please his royal mother, his royal godmother Elizabeth of England, and his Scotch subjects, yet, as each recommended a different claimant for the honour of his hand, it was not possible for him to oblige them all. Mary urged an alliance with a Spanish princess, hoping thus to allure him to Romanism; Elizabeth insisted that he should wed the Protestant daughter of Gustavus Vasa, offering to be at the whole expense of the wedding. The shrewd Scotch people had not been idle spectators of their young king's dilemma. Before committing themselves by giving any advice, they had sent the king's old tutor, Peter Young, to learn how matters stood in Denmark. He was soon followed by Colonel Stuart, and both returned "weel contentit" with all they had seen and heard of the wealth of the King of Denmark, and the beauty of the fair princess. The government wisely thought a naval war with so powerful a prince was very undesirable, and Frederick had ordered immediate restitution of the Orkney and Shetland Islands, should James decline the alliance. Under these circumstances, the majority of his Scotch advisers supported the Danish cause; though, amongst them, there were not wanting emissaries of both queens, who greatly added to the perplexities of his position. Whilst affairs were in this unsettled state, Elizabeth brought her rival, the unfortunate mother of James, to the block; and, before the year was out, King Frederick sent another angry and authoritative demand for the restitution of his islands. Elizabeth, too, put forth another candidate for his hand. She had induced Henry the Great to send an embassy to Scotland, offering his sister, Catherine of Navarre, to King James. Elizabeth urged, in her favour, that she was a sound Protestant; but she did not add, that Catherine was old enough to be James's mother. This inveterate politician sent information of the French envoy's errand to the Danish Court. Frederick, incensed at what he called James's "feckless," or double-dealing, at once betrothed his eldest daughter to the Duke of Brunswick, and doubtless would soon have disposed of Anne also, had not death put an end to all his schemes. The little miniature of "the young Anna," of sixteen, which is now exhibited among the Scottish regalia, at Holyrood, reached Scotland just before the king's death, accompanied by this message: "If you espouse Anna before the 1st of May, 1589, she shall be given you; if not, Scotland must restore the isles." King James took a whole fortnight to consider, and to compare the likenesses of the girlish Anna and the mature Catherine. At the end of that time he called together his council, and said he had resolved to marry Anna. He appointed the Earl-marischal and Lord Keith to act as his proxies. They sailed at once for Denmark; the ceremonial was performed on the 20th of August, 1589, and, in September, the royal bride-elect sailed for Scotland.

Melville, in his memoirs, tells that twice the Danish squadron was driven back by adverse winds to the coast of Norway. "These storms," he says, "were alleged to have been raisit by the witches, by the confession of them, when they were burnt for that cause. What moved them was a blow, or cuff, guhilk the Admiral of Denmark gave to ane of the baillies of Copenhagen, whose wife, being a notable witch, consulted her cummers, and raised the said storm, to be revengit on the said Admiral."

The historian goes on, in the most quaint manner, to enumerate other disasters effected by the agency of these witches, "to which," he says, "they themselves pleaded guilty."

Lady Melville, his sister-in-law—the faithful Jane Kennedy of Queen Mary—was appointed by the King to be first lady of the bedchamber to the young queen, whose arrival in Scotland was now daily expected. Crossing Leith Ferry, to wait upon his majesty for further orders, her boat was run down, and she and her servants were drowned. To complete the catastrophe, the Admiral's ship, in which the bride had sailed, was a third time driven on shore at a desolate part of Norway, where nothing fit to eat could be found. Ten ships of her fleet returned in a shattered state to Denmark, while frost set in so severely that there was no prospect but to spend a long winter in the dreary and barren town of Upslo. Stephen Beale, a young Dane in her suite, gallantly braved the weather in a small boat, and succeeded in reaching Scotland, bearing letters from Anne, detailing her sorrows to her royal fiancé.

The King, it is said, was affected to tears, and at once resolved to go himself to her relief. In announcing his intention to his privy council, he says: "I am alone in the world; having neither father, mother, brother, or sister. Albeit, hitherto we have patiently waited for the good occasion God should offer: yet, now, taking to heart her pains and dangers, we could find no contentment till we bring her home, which we are in good hope to do."

For full details, our readers are referred to the original account in "The Spottiswoode Papers," which are replete with interest.

Fowler, the spy, says that James and his attendants sailed, October 23rd or 24th, in the Chancellor's ship, which was only 120 tons, a mere cockle shell, to encounter the fierce seas between Scotland and Norway: but he adds, "it was well furnished with delicate victual, live stock, pullen, and wines of divers sorts."

After narrowly escaping shipwreck, our knight-errant landed safely at Slaikray: but his troubles had not ended; for he had many days of travelling before he reached the snow-bound village of Upslo,

where Anne and her suite had taken refuge. . . .
"She," continues our chronicler, "little looked for his coming at sic a tempestuous time of year." "When, after nearly a month, he discovered her abode, among Norway snows, he, with the *bonhommie* which marked his character, as much at twenty-two as in his more mature career, waited for none of the ceremonies of his rank and station, but leaving his train to seek their lodgings as they might, he marched direct into the presence of his bride, and, booted and spurred as he was, he frankly tendered her a salute. James had risked his life to come to the aid of the young girl, who had been assigned to him as a wife, and, laying aside the formalities of royal rank, he, at his first interview, assumed the affectionate demeanour of private life." *

On the Sunday after this romantic meeting, David Lindsay, the favourite chaplain, who had accompanied his master during his hazardous adventures, married the royal couple with as much ceremony as the time and place admitted. At Upslo, they were compelled to spend their honeymoon, till, as spring advanced, a courier from Copenhagen arrived, urging the young pair to join the queen mother at the Danish capital. Here, again, the statements of Spottiswoode put the

* Miss Strickland's Queen's of England, vol. vii., pp. 333-34.

conduct of King James in a most pleasant light. Fearing that some opposition might be encountered from the King of Sweden, through whose kingdom they must pass, he resolved to make the journey over the mountains—first by himself, and then, if they proved to be passable, to return and fetch his bride.

Arrived safely in Denmark, after innumerable perils and adventures, the young couple were a third time married, at the old Castle of Cronenburg. Immediately after, the Danish Government made over the disputed islands as part of the bride's dowry; and thus ended the quarrels about the Orkney and Shetland Isles.

Unfortunately for the happiness of the royal pair, other quarrels sprang up, which were far more difficult to heal. On the Queen's arrival in Scotland, she made her state entry into Edinburgh with her two favourite Danish maids of honour, Katrine Skinkelle and Anna Kroas, seated one on either side of her, greatly to the chagrin of the proud aristocratic dames of that city.

The coronation, for a time, set matters right again; and we learn from the chronicler, that, "The stately gear being prepared, the King's procession entered the Abbey of Holyrood. The Queen's followed, whereat were Danish nobles, magnificently dressed, with diamond chains about their necks. Then Dame Annable, Countess of Mar, the Countess of Bothwell and Orkney, and other noble Scottish ladies. Next to them, certain noble Danish virgins, as Katrine and Danish Anna." And so peace was restored. But soon a fresh cause of grievance arose. After the birth of an heir, the King, in consideration of the troubles of the times, resolved to give the royal infant into the custody of the Earl of Mar. Birch, in the State Papers,* says, " the Queen wept, and pleaded that she could not live away from her infant." Finding all remonstrance vain, the Queen continued to wail over her sorrows, till her thoughts were "divertit" by the birth of the Princess Elizabeth. This daughter lived to be the beautiful and unfortunate Protestant Queen of Bohemia, and the ancestress of our own royal family. The same spirit, which led Queen Anne to annoy her Scottish subjects, produced discord also amongst her English lieges, on her accession to the throne of England. We find, that immediately after the death of Queen Elizabeth, James and Anne began preparations for leaving Scotland. The royal progress southward is minutely described, till it ended at Windsor Castle, on July the 2nd, 1603.

Her conduct, after her coronation, appears to have been very perverse, and she, for a long time,

* Vol. i. p. 243.

opposed all her royal husband's wishes respecting her English household. Her quarrels with the English nobles fill up many a page of the history of the times; and James seems to have required all his tact and address to keep his petulant wife in tolerable good humour. Far be it from us to affirm, that in these wedded quarrels Anne was the only party in fault; but it does not come within the limits of this brief history to enter upon the character of her royal husband.

The two visits of her beloved brother Christian to England, restored the Queen's equanimity. As the royal party sat at the splendid farewell banquet, which he gave on board his largest ship, the chronicler Nicholls says, " they pledged each other to continued amity; and, at every pledge drunk, the same was straightway known by sound of drum and trumpet, beginning at the Danish Admiral's ship, echoed back by the other Danish ships, and ending with the smallest;" a happy omen of the present relations of the two countries. On parting, the Danish king's liberality was unbounded. He gave to James a rapier worth £7000; gold chains and jewels valued at more than twice that sum to the Queen's courtiers; his portrait set in brilliants to Anne; and a ship of war, of the enormous value of £25,000, to the Prince of Wales.

A long catalogue of this munificent prince's

presents to the English nobility, may be found in the history of the times.

It was in this reign that the Castle of Fredericksborg, with its fine gallery of paintings, was destroyed by one of the many conflagrations to which Copenhagen has been subject.

The alliance between Queen Anne and Prince George of Denmark, furnishes little that throws light upon the history of either country.

In private life their union affords a pleasing contrast to that of James and Anne.

During the twenty years of their married life, their devotion to each other was unbounded.

Throughout the Prince's long illness, Queen Anne was his faithful and devoted nurse, by night and by day. One of his biographers says, "their happy marriage was unruffled by a dispute, and uninterrupted by a rival on either side." Such a prince might be lacking in statesmanlike qualities, but he must have had much to commend him to the admiration of a home-loving people, such as those amongst whom he dwelt.

In concluding this brief account of Danish alliances, one fact may be narrated of its present sovereign, Frederick the Seventh, which is certainly calculated to impress strangers with a favourable idea of the kindness of his character.

Soon after ascending the throne in 1848, he

made the Palace of Frederiskborg one of his favourite residences.

From being a small insignificant town, it soon grew into a place of importance. A large population gathered around it, and the neighbourhood became a favourite resort of the higher classes.

A school-house was built, a public library established, and musical and other societies formed. But there was no church. It had not been required when Hilleröd, or Fredericksborg as it is now called, was a village; but with about 3000 inhabitants, it was now urgently needed. A proposition was made to build a church, and raise a stipend for a minister. The King heard of the steps his people were taking, and at once sent a royal command that the Court Chapel in the palace, should be as free for all the inhabitants, as for those engaged about the royal person. There is now a chaplain appointed, and the chapel royal is the Town Church for all, who choose to attend it.

CHAPTER V.

INDIA.

> "Come, crown and throne; come, robe and palm!
> Burst forth, glad streams of peace!
> Come, Holy City of the Lamb;
> Rise, Sun of Righteousness!"—BONAR.

WE can scarcely realise the arduous nature of a mission to India without taking a glance at the moral and religious condition of the country at the time when King Frederick IV. first sent the Gospel into that land.

There is one fact connected with the history of Denmark, which cannot fail to excite deep interest in every Christian heart.

In the youthful Princess of Wales we recognise a representative of the king, to whom was vouchsafed the high honour of initiating the work of modern Protestant missions.

A little nook in the vast continent of India was the sphere where these labours began.

It would be most interesting to trace the origin, progress, and decay of Christianity in India. There can be little doubt that India was not neglected, when, in obedience to the last command of their risen Lord, the disciples went "*everywhere* preaching the Gospel."

Doubtless it is for wise reasons that it has not been permitted us to trace, with any degree of certainty, the particular agents to whom was vouchsafed the honour of offering to the nations of antiquity the Gospel of the Lord Jesus. India is no exception to this rule.

We may pass by the statement that St. Bartholomew first preached the Gospel in that country, as being without any solid foundation.

The tradition, which assigns its evangelization to St. Thomas, appears to rest upon the statement of Eusebius, that Parthia was the sphere allotted to him, in the division of the Gentile world among the Apostles. From its contiguity to that country, it is assumed, that from thence India received its Christianity; and hence we may trace the designation of St. Thomas as the Apostle of India.

Another eminent person, to whom an uncertain tradition assigns a part in its evangelization, is the Ethopian eunuch, of whose conversion we read in the Acts of the Apostles. He is said to have preached the Gospel, and also to have suffered martyrdom, in the island of Ceylon, then called Taprobane.

There seems to be more ground to believe the statement of Eusebius, that, in the second century,

Demetrius, the Bishop of Alexandria, received a message from some natives of India, earnestly requesting him to send a teacher to instruct them in the faith and doctrines of Christ.

At that period Alexandria was the emporium of the world. The Church there, if not actually founded by St. Mark, had flourished under the superintendence which he afforded it during the latter period of his life.

From the commercial connection kept up between Alexandria and India, it was scarcely possible, that the opportunity of proclaiming the glad tidings of salvation to the natives of India, with whom they thus came in contact, should have been neglected by the members of the Christian Church. It is most probable that the message was sent to Demetrius by some of the converts, who were the fruit of this intercourse.

At all events, the first preacher of the Gospel in India whose name can be fixed upon with any degree of certainty, is Pantænus, a stoic philosopher, who had embraced Christianity, and who was sent by the Church of Alexandria in answer to this message.

Notwithstanding there is reason to fear that in his case the simplicity of the truth was mixed up with false philosophy, Christianity in the fourth century so far prevailed in India that, in the assembly gathered at the celebrated Council of

Nicæa, in the year 325, one of the prelates present, named Johannes, is described as "Metropolitan of Persia and of the Great India."

The connection of India with the Church of Alexandria appears to have been renewed in the year 356, when Frumentius, who had been for some time in India, returned home, and urged upon Athanasius, then Bishop of Alexandria, to send a bishop and other clergymen to look after the converts, and seek to gather others into the fold.

Frumentius was himself appointed the bishop, and he willingly again gave up the refinements of life in Alexandria, and became a successful missionary preacher in India, where he added many converts to the Church.

For two hundred years we have no further account of the progress of the Gospel in India.

The author to whom we are indebted for the next authentic record on the subject, is Cosmas, surnamed Indopleustes—that is, the Indian voyager. In his work on India he says, "There is, in the island of Ceylon, in the Indian Sea, a Christian Church, with clergymen and believers. In the Malabar country, also, where pepper grows, there are Christians; and in Calliana, as they call it, there is a bishop, who comes from Persia, where he was consecrated."*

The Christians then living on the Malabar

* Hough's "India," vol. i. p. 72.

coast were Nestorians; and it is not a little remarkable, that up to the present time, there appears to be an unbroken link of Christian Churches in those very places, although they do not now hold the opinions of that sect. Buchanan, in his "Christian Researches," gives a most interesting account of his visit to these ancient churches, and the state in which he found them at the beginning of the nineteenth century.

Early in the seventh century, India seems to have been closed against the Greeks and Romans, owing to the wondrous spread of the doctrines of the Arabian impostor; and for many years after the conquest of Alexandria by the Mahomedans, Europeans were dependent upon Arabian merchants for the productions of the East. These merchants were Mahomedans. Many settled in India, and, by their earnestness in propagating their false religion, they made numerous proselytes.

As might have been expected under such circumstances, the Christian Churches of India declined. The converts were persecuted, and many fled for safety to the mountainous parts of the country.

The renowned Ceram Peroumal, who obtained sovereign power in the early part of the ninth century, relieved the Christians of the Coromandel Coast from the severe persecutions of the reigning sovereigns, and induced many of them to return from the hills, whither they had fled, and settle in Cochin and Travancore, where their descendants still reside.

The charters of their privileges were engraved on copper plates. These, after having been long lost, were recovered in the sixteenth century by the British Resident in Travancore.

After a time, other political changes again opened the Indian trade. The Venetians, and subsequently the inhabitants of Genoa and Florence, began to covet a share of the riches accruing from Eastern traffic. Marco Polo's travels to India and China, and his description of the countries he visited, seem to have surprised the whole Western world.

But while these discoveries were exciting the cupidity of Europeans, their hope to share in the profits of the Indian trade was disappointed by the sudden closing against them of the mart of Constantinople.

In 1453 this imperial city was taken by the Mahomedans, and the trade with India was carried on under all the restrictions which had been imposed by the Soldans of Egypt. The important discovery of the passage to India round the Cape of Good Hope, by Vasco de Gama, under the auspices of the King of Portugal, in 1498, produced another revolution in the civil and ecclesiastical history of India. One result of this discovery was the acquisition, by the Portuguese, of several ports in that vast country, where they exercised great influence over the natives, and for a long time carried on a thriving trade without a rival. Another result was the establishment of Popery upon the ruins of the ancient churches.

The great agent at the commencement of this work was the celebrated Francis Xavier. The recent life of this great man, by the Rev. Henry Venn, shows, from the testimony of his own letters, that so far as the conversion of the heathen was concerned, his labours were ineffectual. Those letters only tend to show that the statements of the Abbé Dubois are as applicable to Xavier's proselytes as to those made by his co-religionists. From his own pen we learn the way by which he made the natives *Christians.* The account is doubly interesting, as contrasted with the line of action pursued by the Danish missionaries, who were the next occupants of the field.

An extract from one of his own letters shall be taken as affording a fair specimen of Xavier's mode of proceeding with the heathen:—"On Sundays I assembled the men and women, little boys and girls. I began with the confessing God to be one in nature, and triune in person. I afterwards repeated distinctly the Lord's Prayer, the Angelical Salutation, and the Apostles' Creed. All of them together repeated after me; and it is hardly to be imagined what pleasure they took in it. This being done, I repeated the Creed, and, insisting on every particular Article, asked if they really believed in it? They all protested to me, with loud cries, and their hands across their breasts, that they firmly believed it. My practice is to make them repeat the Creed oftener than the other prayers; and I declare to them, at the same time, that they who believe the contents of it are true Christians. From the Creed, I pass to the Ten Commandments, and give them to understand that the Christian law is comprised in these precepts—that he who keeps them all, according to his duty, is a good Christian; and that eternal life is decreed to him. That, on the contrary, whoever violates one of these commandments is a bad Christian, and that he shall be damned eternally, in case he repent not of his sin. Once again we recite the Creed, and at every Article besides the Paternoster and Ave Maria, we intermingle some short prayer. I begin, and they say after me, 'Jesus, thou Son of the living God, give me grace to believe firmly this Article of Thy faith.' Then we add, 'Holy Mary, Mother of our Lord Jesus Christ, obtain for us, from thy beloved Son, to believe this Article, without feeling any doubt concerning it.'"

In the valuable work of Mr. Venn, already referred to, we find the following striking remarks upon the character and effects of Romish teaching:—"It will not escape the notice of an intelligent Christian, that, in the elaborate description which Xavier gives of his conversions, there is no reference to the divine power on the hearts of individuals. Xavier's favourite expression is, "I have made so many Christians." But such nominal and deficient Christianity can never bring men out of heathenism, or at least enable them to stand in the day of trial. Xavier had light enough to see this. In the close of 1544, Xavier visited Cochin, and Goa, and Travancore, from whence he wrote his annual letters to his friends in Europe. A passage in one is often referred to as recording a signal triumph of his missionary labours—namely, his making 10,000 converts in one month.

There is every reason to believe that the number, 10,000, has been inserted by some dishonest copyist. In three other letters, written at the same time, he makes no reference to the number.

It is more important to pass on to another point, in which his biographers have the hardihood to contradict the positive assertions of their hero—viz., by ascribing to him the power of working miracles. Xavier's own letters do not afford the slightest foundation for the alleged miracles, though he speaks of heathen infants "miraculously" sustained in life till he had baptised them, and of their *then* dying that they might go to heaven *as his intercessors*. Yet the Church of Rome has fixed upon Xavier the reputation of working miracles. It has sacrificed his truthfulness to maintain his miracles, and convicted him of systematic falsehood in order to put his name in the catalogue of Romish saints. Seventy years after his death his canonization took place. Ten miracles, besides the gift of tongues and of prophecy, were then announced to be established beyond all dispute. The former is thus described:—" When he visited people of various tongues, which he had never learnt, he was in the habit of speaking their language with as much elegance and fluency as if he had been born in the countries; and it often happened, when men of different languages composed his audience, each heard him speak in his own tongue."*

* From "Relatio facta in Consistorio secreto coram, S. D. N." Gregorio Papa xv.—Romæ: 1622.

Xavier's own letters tell that he preached through a *native interpreter*. Writing to a brother missionary, he says, "The baptism of so many natives was done by and through Anthony Fernandez, a native."

Again, when he visited Japan, it appears, from his own accounts, that he "failed in the acquisition of the language," and that "all his information was therefore gathered through the uncertain means of interpreters." The truth really is, that Xavier failed "to acquire any native language."

"The fidelity of the 'Lettres Edifiantes,' says Mr. Venn, "has been disproved by Romish as well as by Protestant writers. But it requires much moral courage in a Romanist, to risk the enmity of the Jesuits, by publishing anything to their discredit. Romish testimonies to the untruthfulness of Romish missionaries, might easily be multiplied."

As to the result of the labours of the Jesuits in India, let us hear their own testimony.

The Abbé Dubois, in his "Letters on Christianity in India," says, "Francis Xavier, entirely disheartened by the invincible obstacles he everywhere met in his apostolic career, and by the apparent impossibility of making real converts, left the country in disgust, after a stay of only two or three years."

When confessing this failure in a letter to the King of Portugal, dated Cochin, January 20, 1548, Xavier solemnly proposes that the conversion of India should be taken out of the hands of missionaries, and put into the hands of the civil authorities. He says, "My remedy is, that your Majesty should signify to the Viceroy and magistrates that you confide the spreading of our holy faith to the Viceroy and Governor of each province, even more than to all the ecclesiastics and priests who are in India. In order that there may be no mistake, I should wish you to mention each of us who are in these parts by name, declaring that you do not lay upon us individually or collectively the duty; but that wherever there is any opportunity of spreading Christianity, it rests upon the Viceroy or Governor, and *upon him alone!* . . . I very earnestly desire that you should take an oath, invoking solemnly the name of God, that in case any Governor thus neglects to spread the faith, he shall, on his return to Portugal, be punished by close imprisonment for many years, and all his goods and possessions shall be sold and devoted to charity. . . . You must declare that the only way of escaping your wrath, and obtaining your favour, is to make as many Christians as possible! I can only assert this much: If you will perform all you have threatened, the whole island of Ceylon, many kings of the Malabar Coast, and the whole promontory of Comorin will embrace the religion of Christ in a single year. *The only reason* why *every man in India* does not acknowledge the divinity of Christ, and profess His holy doctrine, is the fact that the Viceroy or Governor, who neglects to make this his care, receives no punishment from your Majesty."*

* See "Life," p. 161-2.

CHAPTER VI.

FIRST DANISH MISSIONARIES.

"Sow ye beside all waters,
 Where the dew of heaven may fall;
Ye shall reap, if ye be not weary,
 For the Spirit breathes on all.
Sow ye beside all waters,
 With a blessing and a prayer;
Name Him whose hands uphold thee,
 And sow ye everywhere."

IT was in the face of these difficulties that the Danish missionaries volunteered to enter the field, where all their predecessors had been so signally unsuccessful.

In 1660, the English East India Company was chartered; and Dr. Prideaux at once made a proposal to King William the Third, to establish a society in London for the propagation of Christianity in his new Eastern possessions.

But that monarch was too much engrossed with his home perplexities to give much heed to the spiritual necessities of his distant subjects.

It was reserved to the *Danish nation* to have the high honour of establishing the first Protestant Mission on the continent of India. The Jesuits had attempted the work, and had, by their own confession, failed. No other branch of the Church had awakened to a sense of their duty. The Danes undertook the vast enterprise of bringing Gospel light to shine upon this mass of darkness; and nobly did they succeed in their undertaking. Their panegyric is thus given, in the animated words of the Rev. Mr. Hough:—" The Danish missionaries were the first to lay the foundation of the kingdom of God in that land of idols; and as wise master-builders, they laid it deep and broad. Their character and work are little known. Their entire course presents an example of piety and zeal, of diligence and judgment, of humility and generosity, of patience and perseverance, of faith, hope, and love, worthy of all imitation."

No missionaries in India were better qualified for their undertaking, or are more deserving to be had in honourable remembrance throughout the Church of Christ.

As early as 1612, the Danes had established a company to trade with India. Their just dealings inspired the natives with confidence; and the Rajah of Tanjore allowed them to purchase the town of Tranquebar, with the territory adjacent, as well as fifteen smaller towns.

Eighty years more elapsed before any attempt was made to evangelize the natives. The monarch who, at the end of that period, swayed the sceptre of Denmark, was a man greatly in advance of the age in which he lived. We are told in La Croze's History, that no sooner was the *duty* set before him, than he immediately determined upon an effort to carry the suggestion into effect.

Frederick the Fourth of Denmark stands forth in history a rare example of a monarch who, instead of using his Royal prerogative as the means of personal aggrandizement, employed it as an effective instrument in promoting the glory of Christ, and the salvation of souls.

Christian missionaries were sent out to proclaim the Gospel of peace in each of the three colonies, over which waved the flag of Denmark.

From that land the Word of Life was now to be preached in India, Greenland, and the West Indies.

It may be incidentally mentioned in passing, that King Frederick's zeal for the glory of God seems, even in this world, to have met with an abundant reward. There is a passage in that Holy Book, which it is so much the fashion in these modern days to depreciate and disbelieve, which says—"Them that honour me I will honour;" and however men may differ as to the *theory*, all historians have agreed in giving testimony to the *truth* of the promise in the case of this monarch. Bell, in his "History of Denmark," says—" Frederick the Fourth mounted the throne in 1669. He found the treasury exhausted, and the whole kingdom groaning under accumulated difficulties. But under his government commerce revived, and the death of Charles the Twelfth, in 1718, put a stop to the struggles in Sweden. Frederick regained possession of Schleswig, with a sum of 600,000 dollars from Sweden, after which the kingdom enjoyed almost uninterrupted peace for nearly 100 years.

Of the three missions just referred to, the earliest seems to be that established on the coast of Coromandel, in the East Indies; and to it we would now invite our readers to accompany us.

From Niecamp's "Historia Missionis Evangelicæ in India Orientali," we learn that, at the beginning of the eighteenth century, King Frederick the Fourth resolved to attempt the conversion of his heathen subjects in that part of the world.

This king seems to have been peculiarly fortunate in his selection of chaplains. They doubtless possessed all those qualities which the nation expects to find in men raised to so elevated a position; but, in addition to learning, they were evidently imbued with the spirit of their Master, and desired that His name should be made known to the utmost limits of the habitable globe. Dr. Reuss used his influence especially in behalf of the mission to Greenland. Dr. Lutkins was no less conspicuous for the part he took in urging his Majesty to undertake the support of a mission in the East.

And thus it came to pass that, in the Danish capital, the King and his chaplains, and a few like-minded men, met together, and in faith and prayer formed this first Protestant Missionary Society.

The coast of Coromandel, in the East Indies, was the Danish settlement, where the first Protestant missionary planted the standard of the Cross. No sooner had the King resolved to send men, than two young clergymen offered themselves for the work. It is refreshing, after the words of Popish worldly wisdom, to which we have just been listening, to turn to the simple story of these young evangelists. In an old black-lettered volume published in 1718, called "An Account of the *Success* of Two Danish Missionaries sent to the East Indies, for the Conversion of the Heathen in Malabar," we have their touching history given in their own words.

From that book we extract the following facts: Bartholomew Ziegenbalg and Henry Plutscho had been educated in the University of Halle. They were about to settle down in the ministry at home, when tidings reached them of the proposed mission to the Heathen. They at once expressed their willingness to be sent, should no more fitting candidates present themselves.

Dr. Herman Franck, Professor of Divinity, and of the Greek and Oriental languages in Halle, was the man, to whom the King, through Dr. Lutkens, applied. The Chaplain wrote in his Majesty's name, requesting that the Professor would select from the young men under his care the two that should appear to him best fitted for so unusual a task. Dr. Franck immediately sent for Ziegenbalg and Plutscho, and no sooner mentioned the King's proposal, than they joyfully accepted the work as that, to which, in the providence of God, their hearts had been already directed. Having done this, they speedily settled all their private affairs, and repaired at once to Copenhagen. While there, they received from Dr. Borneman, Bishop of Zealand, instructions relating to the mission; and on the 29th of November, 1705, they embarked for India in the ship "Princess Sophia Hedwiga," followed by the prayers and good wishes of all who were interested in their undertaking. They write,—"We were dismissed, too, with many presents convenient for our expedition, and then cheerfully went on board, hoping that the presence of God would go before, and lovingly incline the hearts of that barbarous people to us. All these toils ended in a happy arrival at Tranquebar on the 9th of July." Tranquebar, at the time of their arrival, was a fine and flourishing city, fortified with a strong castle. It was also very populous. "Every street," writes the Missionaries, "is crowded with great and little ones." On the voyage they had a narrow escape from shipwreck, which is thus alluded to: "By the help of God we got over this difficulty. The Lord be with us, as He hath been hitherto! May He keep us in His fear, and grant us to walk constantly in the way of truth! May He give us a holy boldness, that His kingdom may be enlarged, and His will be wholly and perfectly done! Hitherto the Lord hath helped us. The Roman Catholics are very vigilant to play us some ill trick or other, but the scandalous and corrupt lives of Christians is our greatest hindrance."

During the voyage they had studied Portuguese, and on their arrival they set to work to master the Tamil language. The difficulties at first were very great, but amidst all they say their "hearts were stayed upon God; and the knowledge that many in Denmark and Germany were praying for them, was a source of much consolation."

The only help they could obtain in learning the language was from the *vivâ voce* instructions of a Moonshee. After a time they became so anxious to make more rapid progress, that they resolved to join some children in native schools. Here these truly great men sat down day by day, by the side of the little black scholars, writing every lesson, as they did, with their fingers, in the sand. It is needless to say, they very soon outstripped their young schoolfellows. By constantly talking with the natives, their ear became familiar with the colloquial Tamil; so that in eight months from the time of their landing, Ziegenbalg was able to speak the language intelligibly. Plutscho did not get on quite so fast.

Before long, one and another of the natives began to inquire about the new doctrine taught by the white Christians. The Brahmins became alarmed at this spirit of inquiry, and resolved, if possible, to put a stop to the work. After vainly trying to find occasion against the Missionaries themselves, they began to accuse Aleppa, their Moonshee; and at length, by false statements, succeeded in procuring his banishment. After he had been driven from Tranquebar, they brought fresh charges against him, saying he had betrayed their holy mysteries to the profane Danes. Hearing this, the Rajah had Aleppa followed, when he was seized, and thrown into prison and loaded with irons.

This was a bitter trial to our Missionaries; but still their faith failed not.

In a letter written at this time, Ziegenbalg says, "Truly all these things greatly obstruct our work. But God is able, by his power, to make that possible which appears to our eyes altogether impossible."

Not only had they to contend with native prejudices, but with the open hostility of many of the Europeans then residents in the country.

Amongst their most bitter enemies was the Danish Governor. He openly defied the orders given to him by his sovereign, and subjected the youthful Missionaries to every kind of indignity. Indeed, the holy lives they led, and the unpalatable truths they taught, were such a continual reproach to him, that in defiance of all propriety, and encouraged by the conduct of the Rajah of Aleppa, he caused Ziegenbalg to be apprehended on some frivolous charge, and kept in prison for four months. The charge proving quite unfounded, the governor was at length obliged to release him, when the young hero went forth with fresh ardour to his glorious work, rejoicing that he had been "counted worthy to suffer bonds," for his Master's name sake.*

* Hough, vol. iii., p. 114.

FIRST DANISH MISSIONARIES. 67

Hitherto the Missionaries had only hired a house at a small annual rental; but having been cheered by the arrival of a present from the king, and also of a sum of money from friends in Denmark and Germany, they now purchased a more commodious building, for which they paid 1,000 dollars. They also opened a school for native boys, whom they began to instruct in reading, writing, and the principles of the Christian religion.

Ziegenbalg having made great progress in Tamil, although at first he had neither grammar nor dictionary, now began a translation of the New Testament. He also wrote several elementary works in that language. The cost of these, together with the great expense of getting books transcribed on the palmyra leaf, for the use of the scholars,—for as yet they had no printing press,—brought the Mission into pecuniary difficulties. They write, "We have neither paper nor leather, pens nor ink, but make the characters with iron tools on the leaves of a tree." At one time the Missionaries were reduced so low, that they had only two oboli left between them.

In this season of trial, when want stared them in the face, their minds were kept in perfect peace. One of them writing home, says, "We could see no possibility of deliverance from this trouble, but we continued instant in prayer, and chose to suffer destitution ourselves rather than close the schools. Both Malabars and Moors frequent our sermons. Some come from far distant places, and put an abundance of intricate questions to us."

The first version of the New Testament in Tamil was subsequently finished and sent to the King. It was the joint production of the two Missionaries, and formed two quarto volumes. Its publication was retarded, as during the time of Ziegenbalg's imprisonment he was not permitted to carry on the work. Soon after a vessel from Europe arrived, bringing money, and what was still more precious, three fellow-helpers. The King also cheered them with words of kindness and encouragement from his own pen.

Imperative orders also came from His Majesty to the governor to render them whatever assistance and protection they might require. This officer was now obliged to treat them with the outward appearance, at least, of respect.

Their next step was to build a church. The one school had spread into three, in which they taught daily; the scholars each learning in their native tongue, whether Tamil, Portuguese, or Danish. But the Missionaries did not confine their attention to their own peculiar work. They took a lively interest in the slaves, of whom there were many in the colony.

In times of scarcity, it was not unusual for the poorer natives to sell themselves as slaves, in return for food and clothing. Many of these unhappy creatures were owned by the Danes. Seeing that no man cared for their souls, the missionaries sent a humble petition to the Governor, requesting that they might be allowed to come to them for instruction one or two hours every day.

Greatly to their joy, the Governor, after some hesitation, complied with this request. This change in his conduct, they felt was owing, under God, to the stringent orders which he had lately received from the King. His majesty had not only sent his royal commands that every help should be afforded to them, but had himself written to the missionaries, directing them to acquaint him with every thing that occurred, either to *help* or *hinder* their work.

These early missionaries seem to have been endued with a large measure of the "wisdom of the serpent," as well as "the harmlessness of the dove."

When they first became acquainted with the wretched condition of these poor slaves, their first impulse was to receive some into their own homes, and by feeding and clothing, to become entitled to them, according to the prevalent custom.

Many parents, too, came and offered to sell their children for a few pice; and the idea of thus being able to liberate and teach them, was at first very pleasing. But on reflection, they gave up the plan, lest it should seem for a single instant to intimate, that they countenanced the purchase of slaves, and thus bring an evil report upon their work. They were confirmed in this determination, when they found that the Jesuits bought up many, at from eight to sixteen shillings a head, for the express purpose of baptizing them, and thus, as they called it, "making them Christians." God rewarded their faithfulness, for the very first converts, admitted to the holy rites of baptism, were five poor slaves. This service was solemnly performed in the Danish church, called Jerusalem. In the old book before referred to, and long since out of print, there is a letter from the Rev. W. Stephenson, one of the early chaplains, in which he says, "Ziegenbalg and his colleagues are laborious and indefatigable, but they have not the power of working miracles, and yet it seems miracles are expected from them. I was never better pleased than in seeing Zeigenbalg preach to a crowd of natives. They showed so much attention to his humble, familiar way of conversing with them in their own language. The Rev. Otto Frederick Kadwitz, a Danish minister who went out to help them, also did good service to the mission. But the reverend the Danish missionaries, acknowledge that their success is not equal to their wishes." The baptism of these slaves, was but as the drop before the coming shower.

Their next converts were nine natives of Tranquebar, and on the same day on which they were baptized, the Holy Communion was administered, for the first time, in the Mission Church, bond and free partaking of it together.

The trials to which the new converts were exposed fully proved how strongly they loved the faith they now professed. Like the early Christians, many literally suffered the loss of all things. They were deprived of home, property, and friends, and were unable to obtain any employment. Neither would their countrymen give them anything in the way of charity. "Everyone," says Ziegenbalg, "that turns Christian, is presently banished from his whole estate and kindred, not daring so much as to come near them again."

Amongst the converts were some who had been Roman Catholics. This greatly enraged the Jesuit priests. On one occasion they collected a mob, surrounded a poor man, who had recently joined the missionaries, beat him severely, and then bound him, intending to carry him off and put him into the hands of the Inquisition at Goa. But the governor of the village, though a Mahomedan, was a just man. He took the part of the oppressed and innocent sufferer, and ordered the persecuting Jesuits to be punished. At another place they beat one of the converts unmercifully, assigning as a reason, that he was a Turk!

Hitherto, the labours of the missionaries had been exclusively confined to the Danish territory. Their fame had now become known far beyond the colony, and many persons came from distant parts to inquire about the strange doctrines they taught. Some influential natives came from the Dutch station of Negapatam, and were so pleased with what they saw and heard, that they invited Ziegenbalg and Plutscho to visit their settlement. Both could not be absent from their own converts, but Ziegenbalg set out in 1708 to comply with their request.

Thus, we see, that a Danish missionary was the honoured instrument of first preaching Christ in the City of Negapatam. On his arrival, Ziegenbalg found that a large number of Brahmins and other learned natives had been invited to hold a conference with him about the new religion, which he had come to preach. Their conversation lasted five hours, in the presence of a large concourse of people, and the impression made by this interview was most favourable, as after events fully proved. Here, as elsewhere, the missionary found that one of his greatest difficulties arose from the irreligious lives of Europeans. One question frequently asked by the natives was, "Whether Christians led as wicked lives in Europe as they did in India?" Our missionary soon afterwards visited the territories of the Mogul, when he nearly lost his life through the bigotry of the natives, during one of their festivals.

On his return to Tranquebar, he found fresh troubles awaiting him. Persecution had broken out with redoubled fury. The case of one young man was peculiarly interesting. He was a celebrated Tamil poet. After hearing the missionaries for a long time, he had become convinced of the truth of the Bible. He threw away his idols, and openly avowed himself a Christian; his relations, fearing that his example would influence many others, determined to change his purpose.

They at first used violence, and his mother even brought a dose of poison, threatening him with death, if he persevered in his resolution to abandon idolatry. Finding threats useless, they used entreaties; and his mother threw herself at his feet, conjuring him not to disgrace the family, of which he had long been the honour and support.

Finding him firm, they went away: but soon after, his house was surrounded by 200 men, and he was forcibly carried off. After a time he contrived to make his escape, and returned to the missionaries, whom he entreated at once to administer to him the right of baptism.

His relations then went to the Governor of Tranquebar, and urged him to prevent it.

But fearing the anger of the King of Denmark, and remembering his displeasure in former cases of oppression, the Governor refused to interfere, and the young man was publicly baptized into the faith of Christ.

His countrymen were now more furious than ever, and even threatened to burn him alive, if he rejected their proposal to return and abjure Christianity. Soon after, he became alarmingly ill, and there was every reason to believe he had been secretly poisoned. At this juncture, a Jesuit professing great friendship, advised him to retire to a French station, to avoid the fury of his friends.

He did so; but soon found out how greatly he had been deceived. Escaping from the Jesuits, he fled back to Tranquebar, where he became master of the Tamil School, and continued boldly to avow himself a disciple of Christ.

After speaking of the faith and diligence of these early converts, Ziegenbalg says, "they all work hard to help us, but great things can hardly be expected from so few hands. After dinner, during which one of them reads to me all the while, out of the Holy Bible, I enter upon a short examination, both with my children and myself, about the things of that day, and then I conclude my daily work with singing and praying." By this loving term, he alludes to his converts, and not to any family of his own.

At the close of the year 1709, the hearts of these devoted men were cheered by the receipt of money and books from Denmark. They also received a letter from the Rev. M. Bœhm, chaplain to Prince George of Denmark, giving them hopes of help from England.

Our next chapter will detail the wondrous results arising from this small beginning.

CHAPTER VII.

HELP FROM ENGLAND.

"The heathen lands, that lie beneath
The shades, of overspreading death;
Revive at his first dawning light,
And deserts blossom at the sight."

A VERY interesting little volume which may be seen in the library of the British Museum, details the origin of the "Society for the Propagation of the Gospel in Foreign Parts." It was established by royal charter, in 1701, only a few months previous to the death of its patron, William the Third. The frontispiece of the book contains a picture of a marvellous ship, with three masts and many sails, and at the helm a figure of a clergyman, with bag wig, and a large Bible in his hand. His face is turned towards the shore which they are approaching, and, from a steep slope, small black natives are exhibited, hastening down to bid him welcome.

When this Society was organized, we find by its first printed report, that its *one* object was— the supplying *British Colonies with clergymen*. A careful perusal of this work shows that there was not the least intention in the minds of its founders to employ its funds for any other object.

Here, again, must we trace the extensive influence of Denmark and her King.

Prince George, by his marriage with our Queen Anne, had become a resident in England. Were it consistent with truth, it would be pleasant to trace any special good as the result of that presence. But poor *"est il possible!"* was not a man of mind or influence. Happily, for the cause of religion, he brought over with him from Denmark, a chaplain, who possessed both.

Dr. Bœhm seems to have been a large hearted and enlightened man.

At the court of Denmark, he had heard the thrilling statements contained in the letters and journals of Ziegenbalg and his colleagues, and his soul was moved with pity for the heathen, among whom they laboured. Using the influence, which his important post gave him with Prince George, he brought before that amiable prince the wants of their Danish brethren in the East. Not content with this, he appealed also to the "Propagation Society," for help. After mature deliberation, the Committee felt that they were not justified in appropriating for *Danish missions to the heathen,* monies subscribed for "Promoting Christianity in *British Colonies.*" Yet, as a token of goodwill, they voted their Danish brethren a present of £20.

This first English offering upon the Mission Altar must ever be regarded with the deepest interest by all British Christians. It is valuable, too, as an earnest of the union, which for so many years subsisted between that ancient society and its Danish friends.

With this remittance Dr. Bœhm also wrote a letter to the Missionaries, which tended greatly to cheer their toil-worn spirits.

It assured them of the interest of English Christians in their work, and held out the hope of more substantial help.

The receipt of this letter seems to have been like balm to the spirits of Ziegenbalg. He received it as a special token of the blessing of God upon his work; and, as means of transit were very scarce in those days, he repaired at once to Madras, to receive the welcome present of money. In a letter to a friend in Denmark, he gives this account of his visit. "Before leaving Tranquebar, we waited on the King of Tanjore to obtain liberty of travelling and preaching the Gospel to such heathen as were willing to entertain it. Madras is distant about thirty-six German miles, which were finished in ten days. One while, I was carried in a palanquin, another while, I was on horseback. Madras is a large populous town, advantageously situated for spreading Christianity among the heathen around, if the English, who command here, would but second our endeavours. I found the letter from Dr. Bœhm, wherein he gives hopes that, perhaps, the English may be prevailed on, in time, to concern themselves in so worthy a design.

The box from London was delivered to me, wherein I found *two broad pieces*. The Lord be praised for this unexpected supply come from England, and for that he hath stirred up some souls to favour the work."

Whilst in Madras he received much kindness from the English chaplain and several civilians, who expressed deep interest in his work, and also rendered him substantial aid.

In a second letter to Copenhagen, he says, "I trust that England, will now unite with other Protestant States of Europe, to convert the heathen from darkness to light."

But amidst the pleasant intercourse with Christian brethren, he never seems, for a single day, to have suspended his missionary labours. We find that he not only preached constantly to the natives during his stay in Madras, but also at every place where he halted, in the course of his journey. In the letter already quoted, he says,

"These Pagans have many fair cities and plantations; and we hope that some will be found, who will count it a joy and an honour to set themselves to enlarge the kingdom of the Lord Jesus in these parts." The Rev. B. Schultz, himself a Danish Missionary, subsequently formed the first Missionary station in Madras, in 1727, under the immediate patronage of Frederick IV. He also opened a school at Vepery, which has been the principal seat of the Mission ever since. Every fresh opening necessarily involved additional expense, and funds were now more urgently needed than ever.

Zeigenbalg wrote both to Denmark and England, explaining that their straits arose out of the success of their work, and again pleaded for fresh help. He concludes by saying, "That promise of God, 'I will never leave thee,' is our one support in our present want and necessity."

In due course a reply from England arrived. That letter stated, that Dr. Bœhm had made a fresh application to the Propagation Society for aid. The committee deeply sympathised with the work, but owing to the constitution of the Society, felt that they could not give an additional grant.

Dr. Bœhm, finding that he could not obtain help from one Society, determined to apply to another.

The Christian Knowledge Society had been

established in London in the year 1699, and the worthy Danish chaplain at once brought before *its Committee* the claims of the Danish Mission in the East. But like its kindred sister, the funds of this Society also were raised to promote religion in the *British colonies only*.

It was therefore proposed by Dr. Bœhm, and carried unanimously, that a separate fund should be opened for the purpose; and the Society drew up and put forth a public appeal for British help for the Danish Mission. La Croze tells us, "Nothing could be more gratifying than the liberality of the English on this occasion. Nobility and clergy, citizens and merchants, contributed to a large amount."

From this time may be dated the close union between England and Denmark, in this oldest and most interesting mission. Every year fresh supplies from our own country cemented the fraternal tie now existing. Mr. Hough says, "Till I had investigated the entire series of the reports of the Society for promoting Christian Knowledge, I had no idea of the extent, the value, or the importance of its labours in India during the first century of the Danish mission. I venture to anticipate the astonishment of the reader to find that so much has been done with such inadequate means." In 1711, the English Society resolved to present the Tranquebar brethren with a printing press—a long coveted and greatly needed acquisition. They also engaged, and undertook to pay, Mr. Finck, an able printer, deeply interested in the work; and during that year he sailed from Portsmouth, carrying with him the much-prized gift.

The hearts of the expectant missionaries were made very glad, and they were anxiously awaiting Finck's arrival, when another cloud obscured their bright prospects. During the short stay of the vessel at the Cape of Good Hope, the printer was seized with fever, which soon proved fatal. The vessel proceeded to its destination, with the press and types, but the hand that was to work them had lost its cunning; and the mortal remains of the young printer were committed to the silent tomb in that distant land, there to await the coming of the gracious Saviour, who will doubtless say, "It was well that it was in thy heart."

Ere long this cloud, like others, passed away. Their Heavenly Master knew what their need was, and supplied it in *His own* way. Whilst mourning over Finck's loss, and their useless printing-press, the missionaries were told that amongst the Danish soldiers, then stationed at Tranquebar, there was one man, who had been brought up as a printer. Successful application was made to the authorities for his services; the man was willing to undertake the work, and the press was set up, from which issued from this time forth a large amount of Scripture truth. The books printed were eagerly sought for, and thankfully received.

But now fresh troubles broke out. The Governor tried to stop the work, and issued an edict that no book should be put in circulation that had not first been approved by the censor. A vessel was just leaving for Europe, when this edict was published, and the news happily reached the ears of the King. Without waiting for a remonstrance from the missionaries, he at once sent out orders positively forbidding all interference with the missionaries and their publications. Hough says, " but for the help and encouragement afforded them by the King and Royal Family of Denmark, they could not, humanly speaking, have carried on their work."

Ziegenbalg, having been reinforced by help from Europe, and being free from his work of translation, now determined to attempt a missionary tour all along the coast.

Just before starting, funds arrived from Denmark, where a great impression had been made by the exhibition of a Hindoo idol of gold, given to the missionaries by a native of some importance, who had embraced the truth. Ziegenbalg says,

"I have sent the King one of the idols, presented to me by some Malabarians, who have received Christianity. It has been worshipped in their idol temples. I have also finished, and dedicated to His Majesty a book, containing the grammatical rudiments of that tongue."

Leaving Ziegenbalg to perform his journey, we must return to his old colleague and faithful fellow-labourer, Plutscho, whose declining health obliged him to return to Europe. On reaching Copenhagen, he undertook the charge of the Society's interests in Denmark and Germany.

He took with him a youth of great promise, who had become a Christian, and had been baptized by the name of Timothy.

This young man awakened great interest in the missionary cause, wherever he went. He subsequently visited England, and was most kindly received by the Danish chaplain, and many English friends.

Three years later, Ziegenbalg himself, finding his strength failing, resolved to visit Denmark, and personally inform his Royal Patron of the state and progress of the mission.

Leaving his work to his colleagues, he embarked with a convert, named Materappen, on board a Danish vessel, and reached Europe in June, 1715. On the voyage he acted as chaplain, and also worked hard at the Tamil dictionary.

One little incident in this part of his history must not be omitted. As soon as the Governor learnt Ziegenbalg's intention to visit the court of Copenhagen, he became much alarmed, lest his own misconduct and oft repeated unkindness should be reported to the King. He begged for a reconciliation, and drew up a deed of amnesty to be laid before His Majesty, which he begged the missionary to sign. Forgetting and forgiving all past ill-treatment, Ziegenbalg not only executed the deed, but undertook to convey it to the King, and to make it publicly known in Europe.

On reaching Europe, he found that the King was engaged at the siege of Stralsand, in Pomerania. But even active warfare could not divert His Majesty from the interest which he took in everything connected with the cause of missions.

The King gave Ziegenbalg a most gracious reception, and caused him to preach before himself and the assembled warriors.

His Majesty then permitted him to introduce Materappen, the converted Hindoo, who publicly thanked the King, in the name of his brethren, for all that His Majesty had done to teach them the truths of Christianity. Before parting, the King conferred on Ziegenbalg the title of Inspector of Missions.

On his return to Copenhagen, Ziegenbalg made

arrangements with the Danish East Indian Company, which proved of great importance to the Tranquebar mission.

So impressed was His Majesty with all he had heard, that he was induced to establish a Missionary College at Copenhagen, for the express purpose of providing men to carry on this great work. The King's instructions to the missionaries may be seen in an old volume of Ziegenbalg's letters. These instructions do him so much credit, that it would be an act of injustice not to give them a passing notice.

An official letter sent to London from the Directors, and containing an account of the new Missionary College, says,—"His Danish Majesty hath received a singular satisfaction from this step, which he has declared in public and in private. We, whose names are under, most earnestly invite all who have any concern for the souls of the heathen, to join with us in promoting the same. Dr. Bœhm is a person very zealous for the conversion of unbelievers. We impart this to you, by that singular affection which we have observed in you to the Danish mission."— March, 1715. Signed, Holsten, Steenbuck, and others.

The King says, in his instructions, "Every member of this Society is to think it his duty, after hearty prayers put up for that purpose, to lay to heart a work of so great concern, and to employ what gifts providence hath bestowed upon them to advance this Christian design— viz., that the Gospel of Christ be preached to the Gentiles, and thereby many be brought over to Jesus Christ. You are to assist the missionaries engaged in this work, and to contrive ways for their timely support. You ought seriously to consider of procuring more labourers to be sent on the same errand, duly qualified for the work. One of our privy council is to be president."

To the missionaries themselves, the King writes: "If you meet with any unexpected difficulties or obstacles, you are to lay it before us, and we will not be wanting on our part to support you with our assistance and protection, for so Christian and worthy an undertaking."

Then follows "a brief account of the means taken in Denmark for the conversion of the heathen." The article concludes with an earnest appeal to students of divinity, after serious prayer and examination of themselves, to communicate with the president, if they are minded to undertake the work.

Our missionary then sailed for England, where he had the honour of being presented to King George I., who assured him of His Royal patronage.

He was also invited to visit the Prince and Princess of Wales, who received him with the utmost courtesy,—entered with him into the details of his work, and promised him aid in its prosecution.

By the Archbishop of Canterbury he was introduced to the Society for Promoting Christian Knowledge. They made him a liberal grant of money and books; and the Directors of the East India Company generously gave him a free passage back to the land of his happy toil. During his absence, Grundler, who was left in charge of the mission, had rejoiced over fresh converts. He was not, however, without his trials; for supplies had not arrived as he expected, and he was reduced to great straits. He had opened a second Charity School, under the kind patronage of the Danish governor, and in four months he found, to his surprise, that it numbered seventy children, whose parents were not only willing, but thankful, that their children should be taught the Word of Life. This, of course, entailed additional expense.

Just at that time, God, who never forsakes his servants, raised up a friend for the missionary, who supplied all his wants till the long looked-for help from Denmark arrived. The Rev. William Stevenson, then English Chaplain at Fort St. George, not only wrote to his own country for help, but generously authorised Grundler to draw upon him till remittances from Europe should arrive. Surely in the last Great Day it will be said to him,—" Inasmuch as ye have done it unto one of the least of these my brethren, ye have done it unto me."

For three years more was Ziegenbalg permitted to labour for the Master he so greatly loved; and then the welcome summons arrived, "Come up higher." Worn out with his almost apostolic labours, which he could not be prevailed upon to relax till confined to his bed, it soon became evident to all around him that his course was well-nigh run, and that the soldier would soon enter into rest. On Christmas-day, 1718, he felt better, rose, went to the church, and preached. Again, on New Year's Day, he felt he must give another testimony to his heathen neighbours. It was his last effort. A relapse ensued, and he returned home to die. Through his last illness, nothing but prayer and praise came from his lips. Again and again, would he quote passages from the Book of God in the Tamil language. It seemed to remind him of the work in which he had been so long engaged. On the morning of his last day upon earth, he prayed with his wife as he was wont to do. Some one quoting St. Paul's desire " to depart, and be with

Christ, which is far better," he said, "So do I desire. God grant, that washed from my sins in the blood of Christ, and clothed in His righteousness, I may depart from this world to the kingdom of Heaven. Christ has said, 'where I am, there shall my servant be.'"

He then requested a favourite hymn, "Jesus, my Saviour," to be sung, and soon after he fell asleep in Jesus, at the early age of thirty-five years. Grundler, only survived his beloved colleague two years. Like him, he was worn out with incessant labour, and died at the age of forty-four, a prematurely old man. While the young missionaries who had joined them were overwhelmed with grief, and the enemies of Christ were rejoicing in hope of a speedy termination of the mission, the Great Disposer of all events was over-ruling all for His own glory, and the extension of His kingdom. In this crisis, both friends and enemies were constrained to acknowledge, that God can remove His workmen, and yet carry on his work.

To strengthen their faith and trust, it was at this very time that one of the Tanjore princes sent a Brahmin to Schultze and his two young brethren, to inquire about the strange doctrines, of which tidings had reached him.

In many of the native catechists and schoolmasters, the missionaries found "brethren beloved," who laboured both in word and doctrine. The training institution ever proved a nursery for the mission, and their hearts were cheered as from time to time, one and another of their pupils came boldly forward, and avowed themselves disciples of Christ. In a volume called "Lettres Edifiantes," the Jesuits thus spoke of this establishment, "We went to Tranquebar, where the Danes have a fine fort. The King of Denmark has a seminary built there, where they bring up the children of the Heathen in the Protestant religion. He gives them every year 2,000 crowns for their support." In consequence of the repeated assaults of the Jesuits upon the young converts, the missionary, Walther, published "A Tamil History of Christianity," a book which proved very useful to the native teachers.

One taunt which greatly perplexed them, was that which in our own days is so frequently urged by Romanists, namely, that the Protestant faith was no older than Luther, and that the Church of Rome was as old as Christianity itself.

By this vain boast, they imposed on the ignorant in India, as they did in Europe. The catechists at first felt unable to answer this assertion. Now, they learned that the peculiar dogmas of Rome, so allied to their own heathen superstitions, arose in the seventh and subsequent centuries, while the reformed doctrines were essentially those taught by the Old and New Testaments.

Not satisfied with watching over the native congregations, the catechists began to travel to distant heathen cities, where, following in the steps of their Divine Master, by the wayside and in the markets, they boldly preached Christ, as the only Saviour. Christianity was thus introduced into Combaconum, a populous district, sunk in the lowest forms of idolatry.

In Niccamp's History, many details are given of the bitter persecution, to which these catechists were subjected. Two of them, Joshua and Rajanaiken, were waylaid on one of their journeys, and beaten so cruelly, that they were left for dead. But as in the case of the Israelites of old, "the more they afflicted them, the more they multiplied and grew."

Hitherto, there had been only catechists raised up from among the converts. Now the way seemed prepared for the introduction of a native ministry. The Danish missionaries seem to have been early impressed with the importance of this subject. From amongst their earliest converts, there were some who had been trained with a view to the ministry. One of their catechists, named Aaron, a man of good family and education, was the first native selected to perform ministerial functions.

He was distinguished by his personal piety, as well as by his talents and usefulness as a teacher. His mother and sister were also converts.

At the close of the year 1733, the clergy of Madras and Tranquebar, united with the Danish chaplains in ordaining this excellent man, according to the rites of the Lutheran Church. Soon after, several others were joined with him in the sacred office of the ministry.

In all respects these devoted men seem to have been in advance of their age. In their distant home, on those Eastern shores, they practically carried out those great theories, which every branch of the *Christian Church*, in these days, unites in thinking essential to a missionary establishment. In addition to a native pastorate, they availed themselves of the aid of medical missionaries, and we find them sorrowing over the early grave of Dr. Cnoll, a physician belonging to the mission, who was suddenly called to his rest.

In the ordination of natives, as in every other step, they consulted their old, tried friend, the King. We find they wrote to obtain his concurrence, which he most cordially gave. He also sent, with an autograph letter, valuable presents, and a fresh contribution in money. But the joy occasioned by these events was not unmixed with sorrow.

Whilst thanking God for the spread of the work, and the favour of their sovereign, they were grieved at the sudden influx of a party of twelve Popish priests, who were sent on a mission, expressly from the Pope, with a charge to "*root out the Protestant faith in Tranquebar.*" "This," says their biographer, "was a commission, which they found it impossible to execute; for they were fighting against God."

CHAPTER VIII.

TRANQUEBAR.

> "Come, for the corn is ripe;
> Put in Thy sickle now,
> Reap the great harvest of the earth!"
> Sower, and Reaper Thou!"—BONAR.

THE Danish Mission now began to extend far and wide. Each year it threw out fresh offshoots, and native churches were springing up in different parts, as the results of the labours of the missionaries and their native assistants.

Shortly before Ziegenbalg's journey to Europe he had visited Cuddalore, a large city in Tanjore, where the English Governor had received him most kindly, and permitted him to preach to Europeans and natives. This visit was memorable, as laying the foundation of that Christian Church in Cuddalore which ultimately numbered so many converted idolaters as its members.

It was on his return home that Ziegenbalg narrowly escaped being bitten by a serpent, whose bite was mortal.

So rapidly did their work increase, and so loud were the cries "Come over and help us," that even with the efficient help of the country-born clergy, they could not meet half the demands made upon them.

Schultz and his colleagues continued the work of translating the Old Testament, which was only just begun by their predecessors. In proportion to the value of their labours was the number and maliciousness of their enemies.

The Rev. Erasmus Orme, Danish chaplain at Tranquebar, was one of their warmest friends and fellow-helpers; and being much grieved at the untruthful and injurious reports in circulation about the missionaries, he wrote a letter, to be published in Denmark, giving a full and faithful report of their work. He concluded by calling upon all Danish Christians to render them instant and permanent help. This appeal was not in vain, and large contributions soon replenished their exhausted coffers.

The next event of note in the history of the Mission was the step taken by the Government in respect to native education.

The new Governor of Tranquebar, unlike his predecessor, determined to watch the conduct of the Danish evangelists, before he took any measures against their work. The result of his investigation was a firm conviction of the worth of the men, and the value of their labours. As a public demonstration of his opinion, he resolved at once to establish Government schools, and appoint the missionaries to superintend them. He then issued an order, directing all the parents within his territories to send their children to these schools. No sooner were the city schools established than their fame spread far and wide; and, ere long, applications for similar establishments were received from twenty-one neighbouring villages. The time necessarily taken up by these country schools drew too largely on the missionaries' strength, and they found it impossible to continue their superintendence compatibly with their other duties. With the sanction of the Governor they were therefore given into other hands. The result was, that the schools soon greatly declined in numbers.

Inquirers still continued to visit the missionaries from distant parts. Amongst others, a Brahmin came from Trinchinopoly, and another from Pulicat, a Dutch factory, and the Gospel was thus carried to both those cities. A little church was also formed at Ramnad, through one of the converts, a Christian soldier.

But the event of the greatest interest, as regards the progress of the cause of God in India, was an application from some residents in Bengal, earnestly entreating that the Tranquebar missionaries would send one of their number to preach to them and their children the Gospel of Christ. Unable to spare one of their little band without neglecting their own work, and unwilling to refuse to enter upon so important a sphere, the brethren forwarded the request to Europe, with a renewed supplication for reinforcements. Many difficulties arose, and year after year passed without the call being responded to. This was, doubtless, partly owing to the unsettled state of political affairs. In 1756 Calcutta was taken by Sujah Dowlah, whose troops demolished the old church, and other public buildings. It was then that the venerable chaplain, the Rev. Jervas Bellamy, the only Protestant minister in Calcutta, was, with 145 other Englishmen, confined in the Black Hole of that city: he was amongst those who perished in that dreadful tragedy. Various disasters came upon Calcutta, and a long period elapsed, during which Bengal was left in spiritual darkness.

The victory of Plassey, under Clive, laid the foundation of the new city of Calcutta, and events occurring in a distant part of India were paving the way for the introduction of the truth into the Presidency of Bengal.

In April, 1758, while two of the Danish missionaries, Kiernander and Hutteman, were pursuing their work at Cuddalore, that city was invaded by the French.

The walls were besieged, and the commandant every hour expected the city to be stormed.

The missionaries, with their little flock of converts, withdrew to the church, and had recourse to prayer. Their worship was constantly interrupted by the entrance of heathen natives bringing in their valuable property, which they thought was most secure in Christian keeping. This in itself was a striking testimony to the character of these missionary labourers.

In order to spare Cuddalore and its inhabitants the horrors of being taken by storm, the Governor thought it right to capitulate: but, mindful even then of the missionaries, he advised them to accompany his messenger, under a flag of truce, to the French camp.

They no sooner announced that they were Danish missionaries than Count De Lally assured them, that, as preachers of peace, they had nothing to fear; that he would give strict orders to spare their houses, and hurt nobody in them. When the fort was delivered up to the French, the Count ordered a guard to be sent for the protection of the missionaries and their property. In gratitude for this kindness they gave refreshment to the officers and men; but being unable to maintain the troops quartered on them, and unwilling to take the oath of fidelity to the French required of the other inhabitants, they retired to Tranquebar; Count De Lally kindly lending them boats to transport their property. When all was ready for their departure, hundreds of the inhabitants, heathen as well as Christian, accompanied them to the beach, where, all kneeling down, they commended the people and the mission to the Lord; and then, with sorrowful hearts, said farewell to their loved converts. On reaching Tranquebar Messrs. Kiernander and Hutteman first heard of the earnest request for a missionary that had arrived from Calcutta. Being providentially separated from their Cuddalore congregation, Kiernander at once determined to respond to the call from Calcutta, and plant the standard of the Cross in that newly-created city.

His colleague, Hutteman, found ample work with the members of his flock, who continued to follow him from Cuddalore to Tranquebar, till 1760, when the former city was re-taken by the British, and he accompanied his converts back to their old home. That place having become a large military cantonment, Hutteman undertook the additional duties of chaplain to the English troops.

In the meantime, Kiernander, with two native pastors, whom he had brought from Tranquebar, reached Calcutta, and under the auspices of Lord Clive, and some members of Council, he commenced the first Protestant mission in that city. He seems to have early won the regard of the hero of Plassey, as we find Lord and Lady Clive standing sponsors to Kiernander's infant child.

The history contained in our former pages has shown, that a *Danish missionary* had the honour of first preaching the Gospel in *Madras*. We now see that it was from *Tranquebar* that the glad tidings sounded forth into *Bengal*. Another Presidency had been claimed for Christ by *Denmark*. Kiernander soon obtained the help of a good schoolmaster, Dirk Steenhover, upon which he established a large school in Calcutta. As the work increased, he was reinforced by Messrs. Kœnig and Gerlack, from Tranquebar, together with Padre Ramalhite, formerly a Romish priest, and one of his early converts. They were followed by Kiernander's son, who had just taken Holy Orders. From this small beginning must be traced the great work, now so extensively spreading throughout Bengal. It is remarkable that for several years, Kiernander's most efficient helpers were converted Roman Catholic priests. In addition to Ramalhite, Padre Bento, and Padre Joseph Hanson, a man of great talent, who understood eight languages, proved most devoted fellow-helpers.

Did it come within the scope of this little

book, a volume might be written in connexion with the progress of God's work in the vast Presidency of Bengal. True, the seed sown by the Danish missionaries was but as a grain of mustard seed, but has it not even now grown up into a mighty tree, under the shadow of whose branches thousands of Indian Christians are reposing? In the year 1789, the Rev. Abraham Clarke arrived in Calcutta; he was the first English missionary who ever trod the shores of India.

The beginning of this work was by a feeble instrumentality. God chose the "weak things" of the world to confound the strong. Ere long it pleased Him, in His providence, to raise up distinguished men, to uphold Christianity and Christian missions in that country. Lord Teignmouth, afterwards Governor-General, Mr. Charles Grant, and Mr. Udney, proved warm friends to the first missionaries; while the private life and high talent of the lamented Sir William Jones tended greatly, during his residence in Calcutta, to raise the European character in native esteem.

The first missionary, Kiernander, was still labouring in that city. For a time he had been under a cloud. By marrying a rich widow, he had been thrown into worldly society, and had lost much of his first zeal. Troubles came thickly upon him, and he successively lost wealth, and health, and friends. In his trouble and poverty, the man who had given thousands to the cause of religion, scarcely had a friend to whom to look for common necessaries. But he returned in penitence and faith to his Heavenly Father, and divine consolations were again granted. In one of his last letters he says, "My heart is full, but my hand is weak. God makes the heaviest burdens light and easy. I rejoice to see the mission prosper. This comforts me amidst all." In the eighty-seventh year of his age, forty-eight of which had been spent in India, this founder of the Bengal mission entered the land, "where the wicked cease from troubling, and the weary are at rest."

In 1799, the Church of England founded, "The Society for Missions to Africa and the East."

In 1814, was forged the first link of a union which it is hoped will yet bind Danish and English missions in a far closer bond. Peace being restored between the two countries, the Secretary of the Church Missionary Society wrote to the Right Rev. Dr. Frederick Münter, Bishop of Copenhagen, offering to continue, in whole or in part, the support, which they had already rendered to the missions and schools at Tranquebar. To this letter Bishop Münter wrote an answer, acknowledging the assistance hitherto given to the schools, accepting the offer of its continuance, and assuring the English Society of a kind welcome for any missionaries they might send to the Danish station. Messrs. Schnarre and Rhenius, two German clergymen, supported by the Church Missionary Society, therefore joined the missionaries Cæmmerer and Sckreyvogal, who had been for some time labouring in Tranquebar in connexion with the Danish Society.

In 1816 the sum of £1800 was sent to that station, from the Royal Mission College of Copenhagen, by order of the King of Denmark. With this money the Missionaries received a very encouraging letter, telling them that the King had taken upon himself the support of the mission, but recommending them to use all possible economy. In 1818, the mission was reinforced by several Lutheran clergymen, formerly employed by the Christian Knowledge Society.

Dr. Middleton, the first Bishop of Calcutta, visited the mission at Tranquebar soon after the events to which we have just referred. He was informed, through the Bishop of Zealand, that the King of Denmark had resolved to place the mission for the future beyond the need of casual help. This was the state of affairs until 1847, when the Crown of Denmark sold her East Indian possessions in Tranquebar to the English. All the moveable property of the Danish mission in that part of India. was then transferred to the Evangelical Lutheran Missionary Society of the Kingdom of Saxony.

The missionary spirit in Denmark was at that time at its lowest ebb. There existed no free, self-sustaining mission. Now a happier state of things is to be found. The Danish Missionary Society has revived, and meets with much cordial sympathy. Its centre is still in Copenhagen, a city endeared to all lovers of the missionary cause by its association with many blessed memories of the past.

The last Anniversary was held at the commencement of the present year, when the establishment of a new mission station in the East Indies was proposed.

Should this hope be realised, and funds provided, there is little doubt, that the Leipsic Society will, in a fraternal spirit, enter into some arrangement for the ultimate restoration of the old mission in Tranquebar to its Danish brethren. Such an act would evince a large-heartedness worthy of men who walk in the steps, and are called by the name, of Martin Luther. It would be a sorrowful thing, that the mission founded by King Frederick IV. should be for ever lost to the fatherland. Perhaps few events connected with the work would tend more to exhibit the true character of the missionary enterprise in the eyes of the world, than to see those who are at the helm of missionary affairs anxious only that Christ should be preached, and willing to resign a sphere of labour as soon as it can be taken up with advantage by brethren of another nation, in order that thus they may be enabled to carry the Gospel to those who are still sitting in the region of the shadow of death. Such an act would be a practical illustration of the words of the great Apostle of the Gentiles, "Christ is preached; and therein I do rejoice, yea, and will rejoice."

The income of the Danish Missionary Society for 1862, was 4,382 thalers, besides a reserve fund of 6,162 thalers, and in the State bonds a capital of 6,125 thalers. Their mission in Greenland has continued under the direction of the State since the time of Hans Egede.

This notice of the Tranquebar Mission would be incomplete without some account of the spread of the Gospel in Tanjore. Before many years had passed, frequent inquiries came from that country, and much friendly intercourse had been the result.

In 1722, a prince of Tanjore, Telunguraja, by name, first cousin to the Rajah, sent a Brahmin to the missionaries in charge of the Tranquebar station, to inquire concerning the doctrines they preached.

Some time after, a native officer in the army, named Rajanaiken, whose parents were Romanists, having had some Christian books given him, was so charmed with their contents, that he resolved to learn more about the religion taught by the missionaries. The Gospel of St. Luke had been lent him, and so greatly was he affected by its contents, that he transcribed the whole of it. At length he, with two other natives, left their homes, and set off to find out the Christians of Tranquebar. He was convinced of the truth of their doctrine, and, after a time, was baptized. Rajanaiken then laboured diligently to impart to his countrymen the knowledge that he himself had received. Three soldiers in the Tanjore army were his first converts. As the number of converts increased, they entreated some of the missionaries to come and settle in Tanjore. The Rajah had already expressed his willingness to protect them. Many obstacles at first presenting themselves, Rajanaiken resolved to quit the army, and devote himself wholly to the service of the Lord. The missionaries being satisfied as to the purity of his motives, and thinking him well qualified, accepted his services as a catechist, and appointed him to labour amongst his own countrymen in Tanjore.

The step he took in thus openly joining the Danish Missionaries, brought upon him great opposition from the Jesuits. During an absence from home, they endeavoured to burn his house, but were prevented by his neighbours. They then excommunicated him, with all his converts and associates. But following the counsel of the missionaries, he met all this opposition in the spirit of meekness, and carefully avoided all disputation. This prudent conduct irritated rather than pacified them, and they exhorted the people to drive the heretic away with clubs. A native officer, and other persons of influence, were so struck with his humble, consistent conduct under trial, that they, too, listened to his doctrine, and embraced the same truths which had made him so happy. Still higher prospects were before him.

On the marriage of his son, the Prince Telunguraja invited Pressier, one of the missionaries, to the wedding, and sent his carriage all the way to Tranquebar to fetch him. Some days after the wedding, he was again sent for, and read aloud from the Holy Scriptures, to the bride and bridegroom and a large party assembled around them. He also gave them an account of the Danish Mission and its proceedings.

The prince, in a subsequent interview, informed the missionaries, that the Rajah had authorised him to say that they were at liberty to settle in Tanjore, and he named two villages where they might erect a house. They were not in a position to avail themselves at once of this opening, but Pressier returned home, leaving Rajanaiken in charge of the little band of converts.

In a letter written at this time to the King of Denmark, the missionaries say, of their converts,—"Amongst those that are passing from time into eternity, there are many, we trust, now before the Almighty's throne, praising Him for their salvation. Of those that are now living, we enjoy daily proofs of a sincere conversion and regeneration of heart."

The visits of the missionaries to Tanjore became more frequent. Captain Berg, an officer in the Rajah's service, showed them great kindness, and lent the catechist Rajanaiken, a house near the garrison, in which he performed daily service.

Affairs were in this state when the Rev. C. F. Swartz, paid his first visit to Tanjore.

The next chapter will contain a short account of his life and labours.

CHAPTER IX.

SWARTZ.

> "Fear not, though many should oppose,
> For God is stronger than thy foes,
>   And makes thy cause His own."

With the history of Swartz, we enter upon a fresh chapter in the annals of Indian missions.

For a full account of the labours of that extraordinary man, we would refer our readers to his interesting life by Dr. Pearson. A brief summary of his eventful course is all that is here attempted. Swartz was by birth a German. Early in life he solemnly dedicated himself to the service of God in heathen lands, though he had advantageous offers to settle in the ministry at home. Like all his predecessors, in the work of missions to the heathen, he received ordination at Copenhagen. After an examination by Dr. Hersleb, Primate of Denmark, he was admitted to holy orders by the Bishop of Zealand. The directors of the East India Company having again generously granted a free passage to the scene of his labours, he and his two colleagues proceeded to England, and embarked at Deal, in January,

1750. During the voyage they encountered a heavy storm, but were kept from fear by the assurance that they were engaged in their Master's work; and that during the century which had elapsed since the commencement of the Danish Mission, no vessel containing a missionary had been lost, though fifty men had up to that time embarked in that blessed cause.

It is not a little remarkable, that the ship in which Swartz and his brethren sailed, was lost in the river, on the return voyage, soon after she had landed the missionaries at Cuddalore. The progress of the mission, with all its details, was not only made public through the yearly reports forwarded to Denmark, but by letters regularly sent from the missionaries to the King, and to the several members of the Royal family, which were transmitted direct, by special orders, to those illustrious personages. From letters and reports now extant, it seems that the correspondence was vigorously kept up on both sides; for in one month, it appears that the missionary band wrote to, and received no less than seven letters from, the King and members of his family. The friendly Governor gave Swartz a cordial welcome on his arrival, and rendered him all the aid of his official position, in the carrying on of his work.

A touching account is given by one of the brethren, of the redemption of a poor child, who had been sold by her mother as a dancing girl, to a pagoda. Not content with effecting her freedom, the Governor sent her to the Mission school, paying all the expenses attendant upon her education. He had the happiness afterwards of seeing this girl baptized, and then married to a native Christian, in a neighbouring village, where she had opportunities of doing much good amongst her countrywomen.

About this time, some Danish colonists left their own country, and settled in the Nicobar Islands, then named Frederick's Islands, after their King.

The government at once sent a message to the Tranquebar missionaries, requesting that some of their number might be appointed to act as chaplains to the emigrants, and also to attempt the conversion of the natives. So high was the estimate formed of their worth, that one of them was constituted Royal Danish Resident. The party located themselves at Nancowry, the capital of Frederick's Island, where they formed a settlement, to which they gave the name of New Denmark. But ere long, the settlers began to pine for their native land. The necessaries of life were scarce, and fever broke out. One after another died, and the rest resolved to return home by the first vessel which visited the islands. Only a few amongst the natives showed any willingness to listen to the Gospel message; and no evidence was given of any spiritual good, as the result. The missionaries were urged to return with the other settlers; but these devoted men resolved to labour on, and for twenty years they continued, under circumstances of almost incredible privation, to sow the seed of life on those inhospitable shores.

They had never experienced any of the *comforts* of life at Nancowry, and soon, they were without bare *necessaries*. Their clothes were worn out, and they had no shoes to their feet. Their huts were so damp, that the mattresses on which they lay, rotted under them. Their only food, for a long time, had been rice; and that had become full of worms. No fresh supply was to be obtained.

It was under these circumstances, and prostrate with fever, that they were found by some friendly ship's crew. A report of their state was sent to Tranquebar, and the missionaries forthwith despatched Mr. Haensel to bring away any of the little band whose vigorous constitutions had survived these hardships. Alas! one solitary missionary was the only one remaining out of all those joyous, ardent spirits who had left the coast of Coromandel. Haensel says,—"Our brother rather resembled a creeping skeleton than a living man." Leaving him to recover from the almost overwhelming surprise of such a meeting, Haensel wandered to the burial ground, where lay the mortal remains of the eleven heroic men, who, worn out by fever and starvation, had, one by one, sunk under their complicated trials.

He threw himself on the ground, overcome by his emotions, and literally bedewed their graves with his tears. Little preparation was needed, and Haensel bore his suffering brother to the vessel which was to convey them back to India.

On embarking, a scene awaited them for which they were little prepared. Bishop Holmes, from whose "Historical Sketches" most of the facts here narrated are gathered, says,—"The parting awakened, in the hearts of the poor natives, emotions which they had never felt before." They flocked from distant parts to Nancowry, and, weeping, begged the missionaries not to leave them; and when, at length, the ship got under weigh, they followed her by the sea coast, uttering a long, wild howl.

Thus ended this abortive, but self-denying effort, to introduce the Gospel into the Nicobar Islands.

But we must return to Swartz, who, by untiring

study, had so far mastered the language that, within a year, he delivered his first sermon in Tamil, in the Malabar Church which Ziegenbalg had reared.

It is an interesting fact, that in Swartz's first effort to build a church, his one fellow-helper was the brother of Bishop Newton, the learned writer on prophecy.

Former missionaries had visited, at times, different parts of the Carnatic, but hitherto, although the missionaries had been permitted to erect a prayer-house in the two villages already referred to, the King of Tanjore had strenuously resisted every request to establish a mission in his capital.

This honour was reserved for Swartz; and, in 1765, under the patronage of Colonel Wood, the brave conqueror of Hyder Ali, at Mulwagul, a church and school were erected at Trichinopoly. From this place Swartz first sowed the seed of life in the adjacent villages. One, called Ratchaumalee, was the first in which the people forsook their idol gods.

It consisted of sixty houses, with a pagoda in the middle. Ere long the voice of prayer ascended from almost every dwelling in that hamlet; the pagoda was deserted; and instead of impure dances, and unholy songs, the sound of praise might be heard, as, early and late, the now happy villagers offered up their morning and evening orison to the God of heaven and earth.

Another place where his efforts met with marked success was Baddalore, a large village in the Carnatic. It was inhabited by a people notorious for theft and robbery.

In 1777 they were all heathens. Swartz, and the other Danish missionaries, felt their hearts drawn out towards these poor, sinful, neglected people, and they determined to attempt their reformation. They visited them, spoke kindly to them, and urged them to begin to cultivate their fields, and to abandon their plundering habits. They then opened schools, and imparted to them regular religious instruction.

So much did these outcasts value the care thus bestowed upon them, that many hundreds gave up their occupation as robbers, and settled down in their own villages peaceably, to earn a more scanty livelihood by industrious pursuits. One of their head men thus addressed Mr. Swartz:—"As you have shown kindness to us you shall not have reason to repent of it; we intend to work night and day to show our respect for you." They adhered to these resolutions; and in a part of the country where formerly no traveller could safely pass, a robbery now is scarcely ever heard of.

"It was a deeply impressive scene," says one of Swartz's biographers, "to see that solitary man, whose only weapons were his piety and zeal, struggling to shed hope and mercy over that vast empire; trying daily to bring some wanderers into the way of truth. The memory of his mother's dying charge, in which she devoted him to God, could never be effaced by any change of circumstance. At times, when saddened by the apparent hopelessness of his work, he would call her words to mind; and then a conviction would come that their fruits would infallibly appear. It was as if her spirit spoke to her son."

A dispute having arisen between the Rajah of Tanjore and the Danish Government, the Danish residents, including the missionaries, for a time suffered severely; their privations became so great, that it was at length resolved to send an embassy from Tranquebar to the Rajah, to solicit his protection.

The Danish captain selected to conduct this mission was unwilling to go, unless Swartz consented to accompany him.

With this visit we enter upon a new phase in the life of Swartz. His own history was henceforth closely connected with that of the Rajah of Tanjore. That sovereign became much attached to the missionary, and gave him unlimited permission to enter the fort whenever he was disposed.

He thus had an opportunity of preaching Christ to all the officers of the Court. One of them having offered him a present, he politely declined, saying that he would not, by such an act, hinder any one from receiving the Gospel. The Rajah subsequently requested Swartz to act as mediator between himself and his foes, saying, "Padre, I have confidence in you, because you are indifferent to money." Swartz simply adds, "But his officers did not wish me to be engaged in the affair, lest their iniquity should be discovered. Thus it passed off, for which God be praised."

In 1799 Swartz received a message, desiring him to repair at once to Madras. On arriving, he was told the purpose for which he had been summoned. This was no other than to undertake a confidential mission to Hyder Ali, to assure him of the pacific intentions of the Government. The summons contains these remarkable words:—"We are convinced you will act disinterestedly, and will not allow any one to bribe you." The interviews between this formidable foe of England and the humble missionary were scenes of thrilling interest.

In the midst of the horrors caused by that war, the vindictive Hyder Ali issued the following orders:—"Permit the venerable father Swartz to pass unmolested, and show him respect and kindness, *for he is a holy man.*" Though Hyder would not trust the English Government, and refused to receive her ambassadors, he, after an earnest entreaty from some of his own people, consented, *on the one condition*, that Swartz should be the man sent. He closed with these memorable words :—" Then, let them send me *the Christian*. He will not deceive me." Whilst at Hyder's Court, he says, " high and low came to inquire of me concerning the Christian doctrine; so that I could speak as long as my strength allowed."

Not only did Swartz address the people, on spiritual subjects, but after laying before Hyder the object of his mission, he spoke to that mighty and despotic prince on the worth of his own soul, and reasoned like the apostle of old, of " righteousness, temperance, and judgment to come." Such sounds had surely never before echoed through those marble halls. The results, the Great Day alone shall declare.

Another, scarcely less striking testimony to the worth of Swartz, was given by his old friend, Tuljajee, Rajah of Tanjore. For years, the missionary had lived on terms of intimacy with that prince, and now the King was about to die, and for the last time he summoned his faithful friend and reprover to the palace.

By Hindoo law, a childless prince has a right to adopt a successor, to the exclusion of other relatives. Some years before, he had adopted a boy, and he now solemnly appointed him his successor, instead of Ameer Sing, his own brother. Calling Swartz to his couch, the dying prince committed the child to his guardianship, saying, "This is not *my* son, but *yours*. Into *your* hands I deliver him."

The infirmities of age did not prevent Swartz from pursuing his missionary work almost to the last. Kolhoff, who had long been associated with him in his labours, was still with him. Swartz had brought up Kolhoff's son, Caspar, and he too was devoted to the mission. His ordination took place at Tranquebar. His own aged parents and his adopted father, regarded the scene with the deepest emotion, and could not restrain their tears. The Danish Governor, and a large congregation of Europeans and natives, were present.

Swartz now felt that his end was drawing nigh. His last illness was marked with peace and joy. Day after day was passed in pain and suffering, but he thought only of speaking words of comfort to all around him. Surrounded by native converts, and his beloved fellow-labourers, he made his last request,—"Sing, Christ is my life,"—"Only to thee Lord Jesus." He faintly joined in the words, and ere the hymn closed, the loved voice was hushed, and his blessed spirit had left the music below, to join the song of the redeemed above.

Swartz had inherited considerable property during his residence in India, and on his death-bed he said, "Let the cause of Christ be my heir."

It is not a little remarkable, that during the early history of the mission, when so few were willing to give of their substance for the conversion of the heathen, a large number of the missionaries were possessed of considerable wealth.

This they consecrated to the work of God. Had it been otherwise, humanly speaking, many of their missions must have been abandoned. They gave their labour, their lives, and all their worldly substance to the cause which lay so near their hearts. The Rev. J. Gerické, who laboured for thirty-eight years in Tranquebar, left £6,000 to keep up his work after his death. Kolhoff devoted his private income of £250 to the support of native churches. Kiernander, alone, is said to have given to missionary objects, 100,000 rupees.

The successors of these devoted men had not wealth to give; but a missionary spirit had been roused in Denmark, England, and Germany, so that funds were raised from other sources. Another peculiarity in these early missionaries was the length of service during which many were permitted to labour.

Fabricius and Breithaupt toiled together for nearly forty years, and entered their rest within a short time of each other. Others laboured for thirty-five, forty-three, and forty-seven years, and Dr. Rottler was spared for the extraordinary period of sixty years.

In these facts, the Christian reader cannot fail to notice how the God of Missions fostered, and tenderly cherished, his infant cause in those heathen lands; and, perhaps, it is not amongst the least of the benefits to be derived from such reminiscences, that they tend to strengthen the Christian's faith in the promises of God; and lead him, whilst gratefully praising Him for the past, to trust his Heavenly Father more implicitly for the future.

CHAPTER X.

VISIT TO TANJORE.

> " And from that scattered dust,
> Around us, and abroad;
> Shall spring a plenteous seed
> Of witnesses for God."
>
> " And still though dead they speak, and trumpet-tongued proclaim
> To many a wakening land, the one availing name."

THE life of the Rev. Claudius Buchanan, by Dr. Pearson, contains a notice of a most interesting visit which that good man paid in 1806, to the Danish Governor of Tanjore. That official, animated by the same spirit as his predecessor, seemed to think it no small honour to welcome a party of Christian missionaries under his roof.

He accordingly invited all the missionaries at the station, to meet Dr. Buchanan. The result of that, and subsequent interviews, was to inspire their visitor with an almost enthusiastic interest in the ancient Royal Mission at Copenhagen. He expresses, however, some surprise at the limited acquaintance which the more modern missionaries possessed of the labours of their renowned predecessors.

The younger Kolhoff, Swartz's adopted child, was in charge of the mission, and he introduced many native Christians to the English clergymen. Of Kolhoff himself, Buchanan writes in the warmest terms. He says,—"He is first in piety, in ardour, in meekness, and in knowledge of Tamil; and his face is more expressive of amiable qualities of mind, than that of any man I ever saw." Going to the Resident's house, he passed through a long street, inhabited only by Christians.

They stood in rows, awaiting their pastor's benediction, while the little ones made their customary salutation—"God be praised."

Dr. Buchanan then visited the Rajah, with whom he had a long conversation in English about Swartz. His Highness showed him the design for the marble monument, afterwards erected by Bacon, representing the death of Swartz, clasping the youthful Rajah, Serfojee, by the hand, while native boys are weeping at his feet.

Dr. Buchanan then, in the name of the Society at home, thanked the Prince for all the kindness he had shown to that venerable man and his coadjutors. He also specially alluded to the support he had given to the Christians throughout his dominions. The Rajah replied, that it was his purpose to befriend the Christians for ever.

On the Sunday that Dr. Buchanan spent in Tanjore, he preached in the Fort Church, where three services were held.

Amongst other facts elicited during his conversation with the Rajah, was the following :—

An insurrection having broken out at Travancore, the Nayrs revolted in a body. The Christians on the coast were the people called in to restore peace and order; and they were so successful, that in a short time the rebellion was entirely put down.

Before leaving a place so full of interesting associations, Buchanan expressed a wish to hear a native pastor preach.

The venerable Sattianadeen, a convert of the olden days of the mission, was the man chosen. His black hair had grown grey in his Heavenly Master's service; but age had not abated his mental vigour, or his youthful zeal. Buchanan's concluding remark is,—" I did not observe that the Gospel flourished anywhere, as it did in Tanjore."

Amidst many difficulties, this early mission has struggled on till now. A hasty glance at its present state, is all that the brief limits of our book will permit.

The Rev. Dr. Rottler was spared, as we have already seen, for sixty years, and was labouring among the converts at Vepery, when his Master called him home. Since then, of the Madras Mission, it can only be said, "What hath God wrought?" A Danish missionary visiting Negapatam, in 1786, found 200 Christians walking in a manner becoming their Christian profession, the fruit of the first missions.

At Palamcotta, the work began through the visit of some Danish catechists; but no teacher resided there till 1771, when a convert from Trichinopoly took up his abode there. A small church was built, and the expenses were defrayed out of a fund left by Swartz. Now the Christians in that district are numbered by thousands.

The present history of the mission in Tinnevelly amply verifies the striking prediction of the missionary, Jænicke, nearly a century ago.

In an old journal of his is to be found the following statement:—

"There is every reason to hope and believe that, at some future period, Christianity will prevail in the Tinnevelly country."

The circumstances connected with the introduction of the Gospel into this district, bring us once more into the society of the Danish missionaries and their converts. Towards the end of the last century, some native Christians from Tranquebar, found their way to Palamcotta, the capital. In 1780, Swartz baptized the first converts.

The mission in South Travancore sprang up about the same time.

We have thus rapidly traced an outline of the Danish labourers and their work.

From Tranquebar, we have seen it extend to Madras, Tanjore, Trichinopoly, Tinnevelly, the Nicobar Isles, and the vast Presidency of Bengal. From Denmark, a supply of Tamil Bibles was sent to Ceylon; and from Denmark, Portuguese Bibles were first taken to Batavia.

In 1806, the Second Jubilee of the Mission was celebrated. From a report published at the time, we find that at the lowest computation, it was estimated that up to that date, no less a number than 40,000 souls had been, through Danish instrumentality, brought into the fold of Christ.

In the Life of Dr. Middleton, first Bishop of Calcutta, there is an account of a visit which he paid in 1816 to the Tranquebar Mission. He says:—
"The further I went, the more was my impression of the worth of the native converts confirmed." A still stronger testimony is given by another independent witness, the Rev. J. Mullins. He writes:—
"Whatever were the deficiencies of the early Danish missionaries, we must remember that these Lutherans were the first to occupy the land—the first to find out what Hindooism really is—the

first to oppose caste. To them we must render high honour, as we admire the fidelity, consistency, and perseverance with which they carried on their labours. They lived not in the days of missionary reports and platform speeches. No magazines chronicled their difficulties, or sought sympathy in their behalf. Scarcely a man among them ever returned to Europe. They came to India young, in India they lived, in India they died. They toiled on in an age of gross irreligion, and they fought their part manfully, and to the last. Peace be to their ashes—honour to their memory!"

A striking instance of the practical good attending their mission-schools was recently given.

A missionary writes:—" I asked my pundit, who has been visiting several native schools, whether he had noticed any *effects* of the instruction upon the minds of the children? He replied, 'Yes, Sir, the effects are astonishing, both upon parents and children. Before your books were introduced, if I had asked a boy during the late eclipse, what was the matter, he would have replied that the Giant Rahoo was eating the moon, and he would have joined others in beating drums to frighten him, that he might let go his grasp.'"

Now, they all know better, and despise the

foolish ideas and customs they once entertained and practised. Formerly, if a boy or man was bitten by a snake, he would immediately call for a priest to repeat mutras (or incantation) over him; and often, when the snake was poisonous, he would die during the repetition. Now, as soon as he is bitten, he puts no faith in mutras, but ties a bandage over the wound, and gets a hot iron applied to burn out the poison.

It often happens in the Mission Schools that the Brahmins enter for the purpose of cavilling. Some of the best instructed boys will at once answer their objections in such a way, that the Brahmins are openly confused, and silently withdraw.

CHAPTER XI.

CAREY.

> "Lord, we are safe beneath Thy shade,
>   And so shall be, 'midst India's heat.
> What should a Missionary dread,
>   Since devils crouch at Jesus' feet?
>
> "There, blessed Saviour, let Thy cross
>   Win many Hindoo hearts to Thee;
> This shall make up for every loss,
>   Whilst Thou art ours eternally."
>
> Written by the Rev. W. Ward,
> on reaching Serampore.

In the little village of Paulerspury, in Northamptonshire, some eighty years ago, might be seen over a small shop door, a board with this inscription:—

"Second-hand Shoes bought and Sold."
"WILLIAM CAREY."

My readers will naturally say,—"What can this have to do, either with Denmark or the cause of Missions."

Let us enter the shop, and become acquainted with its occupant. There stands a sickly, careworn man, prematurely bald, an early sufferer from cough and ague, with no great taste for shoemaking, but with a prodigious power of acquiring knowledge.

From his earliest days, and under the most unpropitious outward circumstances, William Carey seems to have been trained by God for the great work for which he was ultimately designed.

A near relative, in writing about him, says,—"Whatever he began he finished; difficulties never discouraged him. None ever appeared to him unsurmountable." His humble workshop was aptly called by the great commentator Scott, "Mr. Carey's College." He taught himself painting and drawing, and would walk miles to find a curious plant or insect.

A hasty, early marriage, with the cares attendant upon a sickly wife and young family, never for a moment damped his ardour in the pursuit of knowledge.

There seems a strange incongruity in the employments of our youthful shoemaker. In a time of great temporal distress, he records, "circumstances occasioned me to labour very hard, and kept me very poor. I fasted all day, because I could not purchase a dinner." Shortly afterwards, we learn that he was, during this time, making considerable progress in the study of Greek. His biographer adds,—"The straits to which he was reduced were almost incredible."

His business being both unprofitable and distasteful, he determined to open a village school.

And here, again, we cannot but recognize another link in the chain of Providence. We are told that, while instructing his pupils in geography, his attention was drawn by a transition, easy enough to such a mind, from the physical to the religious condition of the tribes inhabiting the regions which passed successively in review. The subject became intensely interesting, and at length was his all-absorbing theme. At a meeting held at Northampton, a challenge was thrown out by a body of Baptist Ministers, whose ranks he had lately joined, to propose a subject for discussion. No one responding, young Carey rose, and proposed for consideration,—" The duty of Christians to attempt the spread of the Gospel among heathen nations." The announcement was received with great surprise.

The indisposition of others to take up the subject only quickened Carey's attention to it. He wrote a pamphlet, containing a spirited appeal to all Christians; and as a practical result of his convictions, he solemnly dedicated himself to the service of God amongst the heathen. His chosen motto at this time seems to have been,—" Expect great things from God; attempt great things for God."

In a letter written to his father in January, 1793, he tells him that he is about to sail as a missionary to the Hindoos of Bengal; the funds then promised for his support amounting to the munificent sum of £13 2s. 6d. In this early stage of his career there were not wanting friends who augured most happy consequences as the result of his mission. Amongst these were the Rev. J. Robinson, Rector of St. Mary's, Leicester; and the commentator, Thomas Scott, then vicar of Aston Sandford.

We have now arrived at the period when the first link was formed, which was to unite him in a life-long bond with Denmark. Friends were raised up, funds were provided, and a passage was taken for Mr. Carey and his colleague, Mr. Thomas, in an English vessel, bound for Calcutta. He took leave of his family, reached Portsmouth, and embarked on board the "Earl of Oxford." When just ready to sail, they were told that it was illegal for any person to go out in one of the East India Company's ships without expressly stating his object, and obtaining the consent of the Company, and that they must at once quit the ship. No alternative seemed left; their baggage was hastily put on shore, the vessel got under weigh, and sailed, leaving Carey and Thomas behind. Next day they started, with heavy hearts, for London.

Carey says,—"On entering a coffee-house a

waiter put a card into their hands, on which were the life-giving words,—'A Danish East Indiaman, No. 10, Cannon Street.' No more tears that night. We hastened to Cannon Street, found that the ship had sailed from Copenhagen, and was hourly expected in the Dover Roads. The terms were £100 for a passenger, £50 for a child, £25 for an attendant. The counting of the cost was enough to damp all our hopes." They consulted London and country friends, and every effort was made to obtain funds, but the utmost zeal of their adherents could not raise more than 300 guineas. This included the produce of the sale of the whole of Carey's little property, which amounted to £18 10s. Mr. Carey and his colleagues were in an agony of suspense. Should his wife now consent to go—and of this there was still great doubt—there would be no fewer than eight persons whose passage must be paid, and this, with the necessary outfit, would cost, at the least, £700.

In this extremity they had recourse to prayer. They then began to bargain with the ship's agent. All they had to offer was three hundred guineas; but the agent, who was the captain's brother, was so moved with hearing a recital of their story, that he consented to accept their terms. The captain was the owner of the ship. No sooner was the bargain struck than Carey, who had been joined by his wife and family, including his infant child, only three weeks old, started for Dover, there to catch the ship in passing; while Thomas, braving the privateers, with which the channel was then infested, took up the baggage at Portsmouth, and, after a twenty-four hours' sail, joined them on board the "Kron Princessa Maria." They simply write: "There, indeed, we could not expect the captain to treat us as other passengers, or to be very well pleased with such a crowd of people, and so little money."

But God put such pity in the heart of this captain that he received them all with the utmost kindness, admitting them to his table, and furnishing all with good cabins in his fine Danish ship.

Circumstances induced the captain to decide on landing at Vizigapatam, whither the vessel had been driven by a strong current. The missionaries felt uneasy at this, not knowing how they should pay for house rent, and other expenses, during the time they were ashore. Hearing them express anxiety about a home on their arrival in India, the captain at once offered to receive the whole party in the house he intended taking for his own family. He also promised them an introduction to the Danish Governor of Serampore.

Carey was allowed to preach every Sunday. He says,—"The men are Danes and Norwegians, and there is much less irreligion and profaneness than among Englishmen. We have a tolerable choir of singers."

On reaching Calcutta, Carey found numerous difficulties, owing to the determination of the English Government not to allow the entrance of missionaries into their territories. He was ultimately led to commence his work at Mudnabatty, an indigo factory in the district of Dinagepore, where he was followed the year after by Messrs. Marshman and Ward.

The bitter opposition of the English authorities made it impossible for them to take up their abode in Calcutta; at this juncture, Mr. Grant, the well-known East Indian Director, advised them to proceed to the Danish settlement of Serampore, about sixteen miles above Calcutta. There they were cordially received by the enlightened Governor, Colonel Bie, who assured them of his friendship and protection. The result of his correspondence with the Court of Copenhagen was a stringent command to afford "help and assistance" to the whole missionary party, and in every way to foster the mission. They were permitted also to travel under the safeguard of a Danish passport. He nobly added, "that if the British

Government still refused to sanction their continuance in India, they should have the shield of Denmark thrown over them, if they would remain at Serampore."

As soon as Dr. Carey heard of the arrival of his friends, he applied to Lord Mornington, then Governor-General of India, entreating his interposition on their behalf. All he asked was, that Messrs. Ward and Marshman might join him at Mudnabatty. But his entreaties were in vain. Through his kind friend and patron, the Danish Governor of Serampore, he was informed, that the British authorities had fully resolved, that no missionary should enter the Company's dominions. It was added, that the Governor-General had declared in Council, that if one of them were caught, he should be immediately sent on board ship. And this at the very time when several learned Pundits and Brahmins much wished them to settle in Calcutta! He had no alternative, therefore, but to accept the proffered hospitality of Denmark, and the mission party, consisting of ten adults and some children, were soon settled on Danish ground, and a commodious house was purchased. Thus, contrary to their wishes and intentions, were these good men led to lay the foundation of that establishment, which under the title of the Serampore Mission, will ever be eminent amongst the most distinguished institutions for the conversion of the heathen. Who can estimate the influence which the wise and Christian conduct of this noble-hearted representative of the King of Denmark exercised upon the destiny of India?

CHAPTER XII.

SERAMPORE.

"Hail sun-bright days, bring on your radiant train,
Peace, mercy, love, assume your halcyon reign;
Arise, celestial truth, in light arrayed,
With beam more bright from error's transient shade.
Shine forth unclouded, and o'er nature's night
Pour the full flood of everlasting light."

OUR missionaries are now on Danish ground, and we must hasten to the end of their story. About sixteen miles up the river from Calcutta, on the west bank of the Hooghly, there existed in 1799 a small Danish settlement. So far back as 1775 the Danes had purchased Serampore, and twenty acres of land adjoining, when Soetman, a Danish officer, had been sent from Tranquebar to hoist their national flag. For ninety years that flag waved over Serampore, ensuring peace and protection to all around it. The Governor had in early life enjoyed the instructions of the venerable Swartz, and the pupil was worthy of the master.

In the hour of their deepest poverty and sorrow he welcomed the English missionaries to Serampore, and never withdrew the shield of his protection in any one of the many subsequent vicissitudes which they experienced.

It was about the time of Carey's removal to Serampore that he had an interview with the Governor-General, during which the question was put—" Do you not think, Dr. Carey, it would be wrong to force the Hindoos to become Christians?" To which our missionary made the memorable reply—" My Lord, we may force men to be hypocrites, but no power on earth can force men to become Christians."

After a long and trying affliction, Dr. Carey's wife had died. He remained for some time a widower, and then formed another, and yet stronger tie, to Denmark. In a Danish colony he had found a home when cast out by his own countrymen; and in a Danish lady he now found a wife. Miss Rumohor, one of Carey's early converts, was a native of the Dutchy of Schleswig, where her father was a landed proprietor. Her mother was Countess of Alfeldt, and her sister was married to the Chevalier Warnstede, chamberlain to his Danish Majesty. After her conversion, she engaged actively in good works, and to the end of her life was a true helpmeet to her husband.

Opposition having broken out when some brethren from England arrived to reinforce the mission, the Governor of Serampore again interfered between them and their English oppressors, and wrote an official letter, saying they were all under the protection of the Court of Denmark, by express orders from Copenhagen. He also stated, that he had authority from the King to grant the missionaries at Serampore all the privileges of Danish citizenship.

This good man's life was prolonged till the mission was firmly established at Serampore, and then he died in the seventy-fifth year of his age, universally loved and lamented. During the night before his death he was pouring out his soul in prayer to his blessed Saviour. He was buried by Dr. Carey, in the presence of all the missionaries, and most of the Europeans at the station. The natives touchingly exclaiming to each other, "Never shall we see again another such master."

For a time the little band of Serampore missionaries enjoyed an interval of rest. Numbers of the natives renounced idolatry, and were baptized, and the success of their labours in printing, and diffusing the Scriptures, was unrivalled. They clung to this little Pella, in which the generosity of Denmark had afforded them a home, and fondly hoped that their troubles were past. But a fresh and heavy trial awaited them. One evening, just before retiring to rest, a fire was discovered in the printing-office, and notwithstanding every effort, the flames increased fearfully. The title-deeds of the premises, and a few papers were saved, but while the last attempt was making to secure more property, the roof, 200 feet in length, fell in. Through the providence of God, the printing-presses were saved, but the loss amounted to nearly £10,000.

The excellent men engaged in this mission seemed to possess one qualification very needful to the carrying on of their work. They thought nothing beneath their notice which could in any way aid them in its prosecution. Thus we find that they erected a letter foundry, with which they produced a fount of metal types, in every language required. These types proved more durable, as well as cheaper, than any they could procure from Europe.

Another circumstance of importance was the great improvement they effected in the manufacture of paper. The paper sent from England, invariably became the prey of white ants and other insects, in the course of five or six years. They erected a paper mill at Serampore, and there produced a native paper, which, while costing only one-third the price, remained untouched by insects, even when placed among English paper already half devoured.

The improvement in public feeling in India

towards themselves and their work was a cause of unfeigned thankfulness. The "Missionary Register" for August, 1814, contains an interesting account of a visit paid to the Serampore missionaries, by the Governor-General, Earl Moira, Lady Loudoun, and the Bishop of Calcutta—Dr. Middleton.

After going over the establishment, they declared that it far exceeded all their expectations. They were delighted upon entering one room, to find it occupied by learned Hindoos, from almost every province in India, employed upon translations of the Holy Scriptures. The Affghan pundit was at once declared to be a Jew, and his name, which he afterwards told—Ben Israel, showed how correctly his countenance had spoken.

On returning to the Governor-General's residence at Barrackpore, the Bishop enclosed in a letter to Dr. Carey 200 rupees, as a present to the workmen.

Through evil and through good report, the missionaries went on their way; and each year the number of their converts increased. Many boldly avowed their belief in Christ crucified; and by holy lives and happy deaths, proved the truth of their profession. In the letters of these good men, it is interesting to trace how much more they dwelt upon any token for good, than on their own difficulties and trials. It is true, that incidental mention is made of persecution from various quarters; of Mr. Marshman's having been burnt in effigy, and of sickness and death in the mission family; but all seems forgotten in the joy with which the writer goes on to narrate the conversion of a native boy in one of their schools. His history is a most interesting one.

At first his mother had not opposed his wish to be taught to read, and he had been for some time a steady pupil. No sooner, however, did she find that his faith in idolatry was shaken, than she commanded him to leave off going to the missionaries. He affectionately assured her that he would obey her in everything else, but he was learning the way to heaven, and could not give up his school and Bible. His mother then followed him to the Mission House, bathed in tears, and entreated the missionaries to give up her child. They told her that the lad was of an age to choose for himself, that no compulsion was used, and he was free to go with her. The boy then calmly addressed her, saying he would obey her in everything else, but he must be a Christian. Upon this she alternately threatened and entreated, and finally said she would throw herself into the Gunga. Finding all useless, she laid a formal complaint before the Danish magistrate. The boy was sent for, and strictly questioned; and as the fact was elicited during the examination, that his relatives intended putting him in irons, to prevent his return to the missionaries, the magistrate decided, that the boy was old enough to judge for himself, and choose the course he would adopt.

Foiled in this attempt, his mother and her heathen friends made another effort to carry out their design. As Mr. Ward happened to look out of his window he saw a boat rapidly pass before it, with the poor lad held down in it. He was crying bitterly. Mr. Ward says, in one of his letters, " I roused brother Marshman from one of his Chinese reveries, and in a minute the whole family, school, and servants, were on the banks of the river. Mr. William Carey jumped into our boat, which was floating by the side of our house. The boatmen put it off, and began to pursue the one in which they were carrying off Ghorachund, while we all followed by the side, anxiously watching the chase. William and his companions rowed as if life or death were depending on their efforts, and the fugitives were not less active. For a time the chase seemed very doubtful; we followed the boats as far as the eye could reach. I then obtained a telescope, and after some time perceived William come up to them, and rescue the young man. A scuffle ensued; but the idolaters were frightened, particularly a Brahmin, under whose directions they had probably acted. Ghorachund, however, was full of joy at his happy deliverance, and was brought back in triumph." After their return to Serampore two of the native converts were ill-treated, and thrown into prison, on a charge of having beaten a Brahmin, when Ghorachund was carried off. It seems, that on the boy's, one day, leaving the Mission House with these two brethren, they had to pass a flight of steps adjoining the guard house, when a mob collected, and the lad was carried off. Mr. Ward at once addressed a letter to Mr. Otta Bie, nephew of the late Governor, and their innocence being proved, they were set at liberty that very evening.

The next steps taken by Dr. Carey and his colleagues, was the establishment of a college for the education of Christian native youths for the public service and other employments.

In addition to English, Latin, Greek and Hebrew, they were instructed in Arabic, Chinese, and other Oriental languages. The poor Northampton shoemaker had not only the honour of having raised this institution, of which he was patron and tutor, but he was now transformed into the learned Professor of Sanscrit and other Eastern languages at the College of Fort William, Calcutta, founded by Lord Wellesley, when Governor

General.* Ever anxious to impart to others what he had himself gained, he, with Messrs. Ward and Marshman, raised the funds, and built the college. It was erected on the banks of the Hooghly, just opposite the villa of the Governor, the Hon. Colonel Kreeting. It received the patronage of the public; large sums were subscribed, and under the auspices of the Governor-General of India, a building occupying ten English acres, and capable of accommodating 400 students, was erected.

On the plan being matured, a memorial was sent to the King of Denmark, begging permission to build on his Majesty's settlement at Fredericksnagore. Not only was this request granted, but the King gave them permission to govern the college, independently of the constituted authorities of Serampore. His Majesty, after having governed as Regent for twenty years, had now ascended the throne. He himself wrote a letter to the missionaries, assuring them of the interest he felt in their work, which he desired to take under his patronage; and he requested them, from

* It is narrated, that thirty years after Carey's arrival in the East, he was one day dining with the Governor-General, the Marquis of Hastings, when an officer present, with a marvellous lack of good taste, whispered an inquiry to one of the aides-de-camp, "If he had not once been a shoemaker?" Carey overheard it, and immediately exclaimed, "No, sir; no,—only a cobbler."

time to time, to inform him of their success. He also presented to the three missionaries the royal building and premises adjoining, comprising three acres, the rent of which was to be applied towards the support of the college.

In the year 1826, Dr. Marshman returned to England, after an absence of twenty years. He waited on Count Molkte, the Danish Minister in London, who received him most kindly. Dr. Marshman next visited Denmark, being anxious to lay before the King the present state of the mission. He then visited Copenhagen, when he obtained from the Danish Government a Royal Charter of Incorporation. This gave the college the power of conferring literary and honorary degrees, in the same way as the Universities of Copenhagen and Kiel; and the property was made secure for missionary purposes. The King presented Marshman with the Charter, richly bound at the expense of the Treasury.

During his stay in Copenhagen, Marshman was presented to Count Schulen and Count Schimmelmann, and from these noblemen and Colonel Abrahamson, aide-de-camp to the King, he met with a cordial welcome and hearty co-operation. On the day appointed, he was ushered into the Royal presence, when his Majesty was pleased to say, that it was *he* who ought to feel obliged to *them*, for having planted the college in his dominions. Marshman then waited on Prince Christian, afterwards Christian VIII., who made many inquiries respecting the translation of the Scriptures, and mentioned the deep interest with which he had attended a meeting of the Bible Society when in England. Dr. Marshman met a large circle of friends at Copenhagen, who had formerly lived in Serampore, and were delighted to renew personal intercourse with that distinguished and able man.

Dr. Carey's work was now done. He had outlived contumely, and borne down opposition; and now, the Master whom he had so long loved and served, sent the welcome summons, and the veteran warrior was called to enter into the joy of his Lord. Ward had gone before him to his heavenly home. An attack of cholera had, in a few hours, removed him from his happy toil to his heavenly rest. For eleven years, Carey and Marshman together carried on the work. Even when scarcely able to sit up, Carey refused to relinquish his labours. At length, the last revision of the Bengalee translation was finished, and he felt that with it, his work on earth was done. His beloved friend, Marshman, was constantly with him. They had loved, and laboured, and suffered together, as none but God and themselves knew, for nearly thirty-five years. They seem to belong to each other and their work. It was a beautiful exemplification of the oneness of real Christians, when the devoted and large-hearted Bishop of Calcutta, Dr. Wilson, stood by the dying Baptist's death-bed, and asked for his blessing. On the 9th of June, 1834, full of joy and peace, William Carey fell asleep in Jesus. Marshman, the high-minded and enthusiastic colleague of Carey and Ward, was now left alone; but he did not long survive his much loved friend and brother. So strong was their attachment, that many predicted that one could not long survive the other; and Marshman sank into such a state of weakness, that it was necessary for him to seek change in the Sanitarium at Cherra Poonjee.

The hot season of 1807 was a very trying one, and it told on his shattered frame. On his death-bed he was visited by missionaries and friends of all denominations, who rejoiced in the opportunity of assuring that much maligned servant of Jesus of their love and sympathy. A few days before his death, he asked to be put once more into his "tonjon," and conveyed to the chapel. The weekly meeting for prayer was being held, and exerting all his little strength, he gave out in a firm voice his favourite missionary hymn,—"O Lord our God arise." He was then carried back to die. His frequent exclamation was, "The precious Saviour! He never leaves nor forsakes." After a fervent prayer, in which he commended himself, his family, and "the precious mission" to the Divine keeping, he closed his eyes to awake in heaven.

"Marshman died," says his biographer, "like his colleagues, in graceful poverty, having devoted little short of £40,000 to the mission, through a life of privation." The connexion of these three remarkable men with Denmark ceased only with their life.

True to the men whom he had promised to befriend, we find that some time before Carey's death, the King of Denmark sent to each of the three pioneers, Carey, Marshman, and Ward, a letter signed with his own hand. It expressed his full approbation of their labours, and was accompanied by a present of three gold medals. The King had previously offered them the Order of Dannebrog, which they respectfully declined as unsuited to their position. The medal of merit was therefore substituted.

One of the latest public acts of Marshman, was to celebrate at Serampore the Third Centenary of the Reformation, in 1836. The King had issued orders that it should be celebrated throughout all the Danish territories, by a national recognition of the blessings which it had conferred on the country. He himself selected the texts to be preached from, and chose the hymn, "Great God, we praise Thee," to be sung. Three days were to be kept as public holidays, and his Majesty enjoined on the assembled congregations to "implore the continued aid of the Almighty to preserve Christian doctrine in all its purity to the country, that it might bring forth the fruits of faith, sincerity, and love."

The remains of all three were laid in the Serampore Mission Burial Ground. They were all followed to the grave by Danish and English friends, and a crowd of mourning natives.

One of the highest dignitaries of the Church of England in India remarked, that there had been but few men at Serampore, but they had all been giants.

In 1845 the Settlement of Serampore was transferred by the King of Denmark to the British Government; but in conformity with the express wish of his predecessor, Frederick VI., he made it an indispensable condition, that the charter granted to the college should be fully acknowledged. An article, bearing the signature of the public authorities, was therefore inserted in the treaty of cession, confirming the charter in every respect.

Although a mere recapitulation is always dry, and in itself uninteresting, it would be unfair to Denmark to conclude this chapter without an allusion to the incidental benefits derived by other places through the Serampore Mission.

Its first offshoot was when the Rev. J. Chater and Mr. Felix Carey, driven away from the work to which they had been destined, commenced a mission in Burmah. The eminent American missionary, Dr. Judson, had visited Serampore on his way thither. Thus began that remarkable work which is the standing wonder of modern missions. The Americans afterwards undertook this sphere of labour, and nobly have they performed their work. Stations were also formed at Moorshedabad, Monghyr, Dinapore, and Midnapore. Mr. Jabez Carey, another son of the venerable founder, first preached Christ to the savages of Amboyna, and then settled in Ajmere, a province lately added to the British territory. Missions were also established at Bencoolen, Jessore, Dacca, Chittagong (where the first pioneer, a youthful missionary, was murdered), Malda, Futtyghur, Allahabad, Cawnpore, and as far north as Delhi; besides obtaining an entrance into the important province of Arracan.

In all these offshoots from the parent stock at Serampore, the missionaries gathered a large harvest of converts. Whilst it is easy to enumerate the names of places which were indirectly blessed through the Danish missionaries, it is a more difficult task to trace the insensible influence of those apostolic pioneers on the minds and hearts of their immediate and more remote successors.

The Christian reader is forcibly reminded of the diffusive influence of the true missionary spirit. Ziegenbalg and Plutscho leave the work to Grundler and Schultz. They, in their turn, commit it to Gerické, Pressier, Kiernander, and others like-minded. Later missionaries are welcomed to Madras, and aided in their work by the Honourable Hugh Elliot, because, when Governor of Antigua, he had watched the noble and consistent conduct of other brethren labouring in that island. Carey and his colleagues are welcome to Serampore, because Colonel Bie had learnt the religion of Jesus from Swartz. Judson goes to Burmah, and Henry Martyn to Persia, after having been strengthened and refreshed by the Serampore missionaries. And so we may trace the "succession" down to the present day. Of each one, as he passed away to his home in the skies, may it be said, "He being dead yet speaketh!" The case of a convert at Monghyr is referred to as a specimen. The man's name was Bindabund; he was a noted character in the district, having been for many years a religious mendicant; his hair and beard had been untouched for years, and his whole appearance was most revolting. Attracted by the report of others, he one day drew near to the crowd in a fair, and for the first time heard the way of salvation, through simple faith in Christ Jesus. He at once received the Gospel, and found that it was indeed the "power of God unto salvation." From that time he became a new man. He went to Mr. Chamberlain, the missionary, and said, in allusion to the Eastern custom of presenting flowers, "I have a flower (meaning his heart) which I wish to give to some one who is worthy of it. For many years I have gone about the country to find such a person, but in vain. I have been to Juggernaut, but there I saw only a piece of wood. That was not worthy of it; but to-day I have found one that is, and He shall have it. Jesus Christ is worthy of my flower."

He soon began to declare the Gospel to his heathen countrymen, spending his entire time in reading the Scriptures, and telling them of the Saviour who had made him so happy. Five years were thus spent, during which he would walk from twenty to thirty miles a day, without remuneration, to tell others of the treasure he had found. When dying, he was asked if he would take anything, when, laying his hand on a portion of the Scriptures which lay near him, he said, "This is my meat, drink, and medicine." As his neighbours stood around his door he repeated portions from the Word of God from memory, and prayed, though able only to utter a few words at a time. The next day, when they came, he was gone home, to the Saviour whom he loved.

Not content with these efforts in Bengal, Dr. Carey and Mr. Thomas made an attempt to take the Gospel into Bhootan, a large province of Northern Hindoostan, bordering on Thibet. The missionaries, on their first visit, met with much kindness. The Soobah, a kind of viceroy, who received them, presented them with a white silk scarf, in the name of the Grand Lama, and one of red silk from himself. The Soobah then invited the missionaries to his own house, which they reached by ascending a ladder. He led them into his large reception room, and seated them by his side, on his own elevated seat, at the end of the apartment, which was covered with red cloth, and hung round with thin gauze curtains; and insisted, with great generosity, in providing for their wants. After partaking of refreshment, they told him the object of their visit, and had much conversation with him respecting the Gospel. He spoke to them with great politeness, addressing them as Lama, or teacher. When informed that they had no present intention of remaining, as their object had only been to ascertain the willingness of the Bhootans to receive a missionary when one could be sent, the Soobah dismissed them with bands of music, and sent guides to conduct them on their homeward way. This took place in 1797. It was not till 1809 that any of the missionary party could be spared from Serampore to make a second visit to Bhootan; and this time it was with the view of forming a settlement. Mr. William Carey, jun., third son of the venerable founder of the Serampore Mission, now felt determined to go, and make an attempt to settle amongst the people who had so cordially welcomed his father. He was accompanied by Mr. Robinson, who had but recently arrived from England.

After a long and fatiguing journey on horseback, they reached Barbaree, and then hastened on to Bote-Haut, where they waited on the chief magistrate, and told him of their wish to secure a piece of ground on which to build a house. He sent them a most courteous reply, in these words: —" Come and stay with me a few days, and tell me your joys and sorrows."

On arriving they met with a cordial reception from the Katma, the official in residence, and were received into his friendship—an act which, in that country, is accompanied by peculiar ceremonies. A spot of ground was promised them, on which to build a house. Mr. Robinson, through undue exposure to the sun, was seized with fever, and the two native converts who had accompanied them from Serampore were also taken ill. In a short time they all recovered, and everything seemed going on prosperously. A small native house was built; and twice a week, on market days, the missionaries proclaimed the truth to a large number of persons. But, to quote a text to which they often referred, "We know not what a day may bring forth."

One night after the weary missionaries had retired to rest, their premises were attacked by an armed band of fifty or sixty robbers. They entered the mission house, and carried off all the property of every kind that the missionaries possessed. Feeling that they must be overpowered by numbers, the two brethren and their helpers thought only of escape. But Mr. Robinson in the attempt received four wounds, one of which, in his breast, would have proved mortal, had not the spear providentially struck against the bone. His companion escaped with only one severe wound in the side. In this state of suffering, and with scarcely any clothing, they travelled for three days, till worn out with pain and hunger, they reached Dinagepore. Here kind friends were raised up who received them into their house, until able to return to their loved home at Serampore. Thus for the present ended the attempt to establish a mission in Bhootan. A mission to Sirdhana, near Meerut, in the North West provinces, was also undertaken by Mr. Chamberlain, another of the Serampore missionaries. This small feudal territory is noted as having been once governed by the famous Begum Sumroo.

In this short review of the past, it is impossible not to contrast the present wide-spread field open before every Christian labourer, with the days, scarcely more than a generation ago, when our so-called Christian Government systematically refused permission to any missionary to set foot in India, and openly patronized the worst form of heathen idolatry. Does it not behove every follower of Christ to "thank God, and take courage?"

Many of these spheres of labour are now occupied by devoted missionaries in connexion with different societies, who are uniting to pull down the strongholds of Heathenism.

CHAPTER XIII.

BOMBAY AND A DANISH SEAMAN.

> "A nameless man amid a crowd,
> That thronged the daily mart,
> Let fall a word of Hope and Love,
> Unstudied from the heart;
> A whisper on the tumult thrown—
> A transitory breath.
> It raised a brother from the dust,
> It saved a soul from death!
> O germ! O fount! O word of love!
> O thought at random cast!
> Ye were but little at the first,
> But mighty at the last!

It has already been shown how largely the presidencies of Madras and Bengal were indebted to Denmark.

Bombay, though in a less degree, shared in the blessings which the Tranquebar mission brought in its train.

The earliest record of the Gospel being preached in Bombay is in 1714, when the Rev. Richard Cobbe was appointed first chaplain to Fort St. George.

From the "Life of the Rev. Henry Martyn," we learn that he visited Bombay on his route to Shiraz. There is in that life a letter written from Bombay, containing the following reflections:

"I am here amongst men who are without God in the world. How insensible are men of the world to all that God is doing! How unconscious of His purposes concerning His Church! How incapable seemingly of comprehending the existence of it!"

He preached five times, held conversations with learned natives, had discussions with a zealous Parsee, and a Mussulman, and doubtless his visit prepared the way for those who were shortly to follow. As early as 1804, the London Missionary Society resolved to send a minister into that presidency, but three years elapsed before a suitable man was found.

Owing to the differences which then existed between the Governments of Great Britain and the United States, many difficulties arose in the way of any missionary sailing by way of America. Dr. Taylor, the young missionary who was the first chosen, was a physician. Instead of proceeding at once to Western India, as intended, he accompanied the vessel, in which he was a passenger, to Bengal. Hence arose his connection with the Serampore missions. Finding Dr. Carey and his friends so happily settled under Danish protection, he joined their party, and set diligently to work to master Hindustani, and Mahratta. Under their teaching he gained a considerable insight into these languages, and also learned something of Persian. Thus prepared for his work, beneath the sheltering flag of Denmark, he took leave of the veterans at Serampore, and sailed for Bombay in 1807. He found many difficulties in his way, and was at length induced to accept a medical appointment under Government. His two successors came direct from England, but went to reside at Surat. Here, strange to say, they formed another link with Denmark. At first they had some difficulty in fixing on a suitable home; but they finally took up their abode with Mr. Aratoon, an Armenian convert, who had been associated with the brethren at Serampore. Subsequently, a party of five missionaries sailed from America for Serampore, in 1812. On their reaching Calcutta, the Governor-General issued an order that they should all return by the vessel which had brought them. To this was added a statement that only £40 would be allowed for their passage, and that they should mess with the gunner. No notice was taken of their wives; and it was evidently a matter of indifference to the Government, if they were left behind to starve.

Two of the number, Messrs. Hall and Nott, contrived to steal down the river in a boat, and escaped to Bombay.

Thus again, as in many previous instances, did the wrath of man turn out for the furtherance of the Gospel.

From these small beginnings, we trace the present extended work in the presidency of Bombay, to which it is not within the compass of this work to make further allusion.

There are still to be found in Denmark, men of a like spirit with those whose history we have been contemplating.

A touching account has lately been published by an Arctic traveller, of a noble-hearted sailor, who seems as deeply imbued with a missionary spirit as some of his more illustrious countrymen.

The simple story is as follows :—An exploring party having been formed, a Danish seaman volunteered his services as interpreter. Having lived in various parts of Greenland, and knowing the people and the language, he was admirably fitted for the post. He was, to use his own language, a God-fearing man ; and while on board ship with the narrator of this story, he certainly proved that he knew no other fear. This man had a wife and children in Denmark, to whom he seemed tenderly attached.

On being asked how he could leave them for such a dangerous service, he told the following simple tale :—

"From my childhood I had a great desire to become a minister, but my friends were poor, and could not afford the expense, so I was forced to learn a trade.

"But so strong was my desire to become a missionary, that I attached myself to a minister, going to one of the Greenland settlements.

"Liefly was the first spot I lived at.

"For many years I lived among the Esquimaux, who inhabit the most northern parts, and assisted to teach them the knowledge of the Saviour and of the Bible, so that I gradually learnt their language. About this time I married.

"I then resolved, should God bless me with a son, to dedicate him to His service, if I could by any means save money enough to have him educated.

"At last I became a parent.

"How joyful I then was! How I thanked my Maker for His goodness to me! I strove harder than ever to get on; but alas! in this out-of-the-way part of the world, I could earn but little. However, I prayed to God to help me, and bless my purpose. I heard of the *whale fishery islands*, where English ships came out to look for Sir John Franklin; and my old master, the Moravian missionary, wrote to me, and asked me if I would like to go with them as interpreter, as by that means I might earn enough to carry out my wish. Before this, I must tell you, my wife fell sick, and I sent her back to Denmark with my children.

"At first it seemed very hard to have to part with them, but now I see that it was all wisely ordered. In Denmark, my boy would be taught, and so I felt nearer to my object than ever, and more happy.

"This is the reason why I am away from my wife and children: but I feel that God will bless my undertaking, and therefore gladly deny myself little comforts to forward my wishes. I heard from my boy by the last ship from Denmark, and they say that he is very quick at learning, and will make a good minister. I have nearly saved enough to ensure his being a missionary; and when that is accomplished, with God's will, I hope to return to my family, never again to leave them.

"I have served in many ships, and have been alone in many long land journeys, but there is one who travels with me, and who is a certain companion—my Saviour. I have never ceased to pray for help to carry out my intention, and if I am not too presumptuous, I think my prayer has been heard; for never was a man more fortunate than myself, since my first struggle to lay by a sum sufficient to educate my boy." This was the ambition of his life. And surely a nobler one could not be found than that of giving his first born to the cause of Christ, to promote the salvation of the souls of these poor children of barren Greenland.

CHAPTER XIV.

GREENLAND.

"Be not weary, toiling Christian, good the Master thou dost serve;
Let no disappointment move thee; from thy service never swerve.
Sow in hope, nor cease thy sowing, lack not patience, faith, or prayer.
Seed-time passeth,—harvest hasteneth, precious sheaves thou then shalt bear."

THE zeal of Danish Christians was not satisfied when they had sown the seed of Gospel truth on the Coromandel coast. Frederick IV. acted as a sovereign who felt that he must one day render an account to the King of kings, and he gladly gave all the weight of his exalted station to aid any of his subjects in endeavouring to spread the truth.

This was remarkably evident in all he did with reference to the introduction of the Gospel into Greenland. For the whole details of this mission, we are indebted either to the valuable and scarce volumes of Crantz, or to the work of Hans Egede himself, dedicated to his beloved and Royal Patron.

Greenland is well known as the most northern tract of land between Europe and the main continent of America. For a long period it was thought to be a peninsula, but modern discoveries have led to the conclusion that it is a large island, or rather a vast group of islands, compacted by the ice, so as to resemble a continuous tract of land. No satisfactory proofs exist that Greenland was inhabited before the arrival of its Scandinavian discoverers. The earliest notices of the country, are to be found in the "Iceland Chronicles," by that very ancient historian, Sturlesen, who fixes its discovery about 982. Another writer, Christophersen, who enlarges much, in Danish verse, on the icy beauties of this new-found land, affirms 770 to be the true date of its discovery.

The Iceland Chronicle tells us that Greenland became tributary to the King of Norway, A.D. 1023; after which a long time elapsed, "in which the country was no more remembered." The name of Greenland was given by its discoverers on account of its verdant appearance. But the east and verdant side, which was that first seen, is at present unknown, having been for years unapproachable through the prodigious masses of ice constantly floating by; hence that part is called *ancient*, or *lost* Greenland. In 1389 it was determined to send some merchants to Greenland, but many of the vessels perished in storms, and after a heavy loss of human lives and treasure, the attempt was given up as fruitless. The first traders from Denmark reached Greenland about the year 1605, but on returning home, the ship was lost, and every soul on board perished. Another party sent out by Christian II. in the year following, lost half her cargo and many of her crew. Still later, other fruitless attempts were made to establish a colony. Notwithstanding these repeated failures, in 1636 a company of Copenhagen merchants fitted out two vessels at great expense. They arrived in safety, and speedily began to barter with the natives. Whilst so engaged, one of the sailors noticed on the beach a kind of sand of a golden colour, and very heavy. The crew at once jumped to the conclusion that they had discovered another Ophir. The trade in seals and blubber was speedily abandoned, and both the ships were filled with the precious treasure. When examined on their return to Copenhagen, it was found to be nothing but sand, and the ship loads had to be thrown into the sea. After these repeated failures, the spirit of northern enterprise died away. It was reserved for Frederick IV. of Denmark to obtain a permanent footing on those cold and distant shores; and that solid footing was obtained through the introduction of Christianity.

We have already seen how anxious the Danes were to search out and repossess this long lost land of their ancestors. The person whom God raised up to undertake this difficult and self-denying work, was a man eminently fitted for the task. Everything connected with this remarkable missionary is so peculiar, that we venture to give rather a circumstantial narrative of his early history. For a fuller account the writer would refer to his Life, in her little volume "Toils and Triumphs."

Hans Egede, the originator of the Greenland Mission, was the youthful pastor of Vogen, in Norway. When a child, he had delighted to listen to the mysterious legends of his fatherland. Amongst them, one was indelibly fixed in his memory. The tradition was, that several centuries before, two Venetians of rank had embarked on a distant voyage. That a storm had arisen which drove them to the shores of Greenland, where they found whole villages inhabited by Christians. As years passed on, Egede dwelt more and more on the wondrous tale. What if it were true? How glorious and noble the errand, to seek out these long-neglected Christians, and carry to them the consolations of the Gospel. Again and again he strove to banish the thought, but it was in vain. At length, he could no longer withstand the impulse, and after making known his feelings to his bishop, he resolved to prosecute the matter in person: he repaired to Copenhagen. On his arrival at Copenhagen, he earnestly requested an interview with the King. This was granted; when he unfolded to His Majesty the yearnings of his soul over the benighted inhabitants of Greenland, and besought his help in carrying out his plans. One serious obstacle was the difficulty which the King foresaw in raising money, as Denmark was then involved in a war with Sweden. His Majesty, however, was so struck with the statements of Egede, that he commanded instant inquiries to be made of the captains and pilots who had at any time been engaged in the whale fishery, that he might himself form an opinion as to their willingness to renew the trade, and thus secure an opening for the Gospel. But so disinclined were these men to risk a repetition of the hardships they had undergone in their casual visits, that they retracted all their former statements, fearful of being ordered away on an exploring expedition, should their accounts be at all of a favourable nature.

Hitherto, his wife had opposed the undertaking; but she was at length brought heartily to co-operate with her husband in his endeavours to carry out his beloved project. But opposition sprang up on every side. Some tried to divert him from his purpose by urging the miseries and suffering he would inflict on those most dear to him; others accused him of sinister motives, charged him with ambitious views, and even asserted that he aimed only at temporal emolument. Others, who gave themselves credit for great charity, pitied him as a mad fanatic, hardly fit to be trusted with the lives of his wife and children.

Meantime, a report reached Copenhagen, that a ship from Bergen had been wrecked in the Greenland seas, and the whole of the crew murdered and eaten. Nothing daunted, Egede continued to urge the subject upon all within his reach, till the King, touched by his zeal, resolved to undertake the mission.

The death of Charles the Twelfth, in the following year, gave hopes of peace; and King Frederick sent Egede a most gracious message to the effect, that if his heart was still set upon attempting to convert the Greenlanders, he would publicly show his approval of the undertaking by giving him a salary of three hundred rix dollars a year.

The King afterwards honoured him with another interview, when he attentively heard all Egede's proposals, after which, he added a present of 200 rix dollars more, towards his outfit.

Thus, after a patient struggle of thirteen years, Egede attained the prospect of carrying out his undertaking. A vessel called the "Hope" was purchased, and, accompanied by prayers and good wishes, he embarked with his family and a number of settlers, in May, 1720. After a three weeks' sail, their progress was checked by icebergs. The vessel sprang a leak, and the captain, rushing into the missionary's cabin, told him they must all prepare for instant death, as there was no hope of escape.

The feelings of Egede on this occasion are more easy to conceive than to describe; but God's providence was over them. A fog arose, and by morning, the quantity of ice was so inconsiderable, that they could scarcely believe they had been in such imminent danger. In the course of the day, the vessel was free again; and on the 3rd of July, 1721, they landed, and immediately began to erect a house of turf and stone.

At first, the natives were friendly; but when they found that the strangers were making preparations to stay, they showed great dread. They could not conceive that Europeans could come for any other purpose than to revenge the death of their countrymen. Many struck their tents, and went to a distant part of the island: but in time, their fears subsided, and they grew friendly with the stranger, who, they said, was himself an angekok, or priest. Egede lost no opportunity of learning the language. As soon as he heard the word *Kina*—" What is this ? " he asked the name of everything around him. Until he was able to talk with them, he tried to instruct them through pictures, illustrating great Scripture facts —as the Fall, and the Death and Resurrection of Christ.

The following year, a fresh trial awaited him. No vessel from home had arrived, and the store of food was nearly exhausted. Only some biscuits, oatmeal, and three barrels of peas were left, and this to support thirty people ! At this crisis, he says, " my only hope was from my Father in heaven ; my only earthly comfort, the fortitude and unshaken faith of my wife." Just at this time, Frederick the Fourth, who was a noble and large-hearted monarch, unwilling to abandon the man whom he had promised to protect, sent out ships with fresh supplies. In the " description of Greenland," by Hans Egede, we have interesting details of the heartiness with which the King entered into that great missionary's work.

Egede seems to have spared no pains to excite a similar interest in the spread of Christ's kingdom in the heart of the young hereditary Prince of Denmark. In dedicating to him a work upon

Missions, he uses the following language :—" May it please your Royal Highness. As I took the freedom humbly to address to the King, your Royal father, an account of the Greenland Mission's beginning and propagation, which His Majesty, with so glorious a zeal, protects and encourages; so likewise, with the same most humble submission, I offer to your Royal Highness this present survey of Greenland, endeavouring by this means to insinuate and recommend to your Royal Highness's favour and protection, so pious an undertaking. This little work cannot fail of a gracious reception from your Royal Highness, as it aims only at, and is calculated for, the honour of God, and your Royal family's exaltation; *the last of which wholly depends on, and necessarily follows, the first:* for when the poor Greenlanders shall have learnt to know and worship God as their Creator and Redeemer, *then* will they likewise learn to acknowledge and honour a Christian Sovereign as their King and Ruler, through whose most Christian care and beneficence, they have been brought to the knowledge of salvation."

In the preface to his work, Egede writes thus :—

"It is confessed that Greenland is a country not unworthy the keeping and improving. This has been the well-grounded opinion of our late monarchs of Denmark; and many of their chief counsellors, who have made so much of Greenland, chiefly to the end that the Christian religion may be re-established, and the poor inhabitants—the offspring of the old Northern Christians (if through God's mercy any such may yet be found) might be assisted and comforted both as to body and soul. That God in his mercy may advance and promote this, my well-meant project, to the honour of His most Holy Name, and the enlightening and saving of these poor souls, is the sincere desire of *Hans Egede.*"

The description our missionary then proceeds to give of the people in his charge, is such as could not now be reprinted. The habits of the natives were so repulsive, that even the rough sailors could not tolerate a residence amongst them.

When the supplies failed from the fatherland, Egede, with his delicate young wife, and four little children, often had nothing but native food to eat. This, he tells us, consisted of fish and flesh meat, sometimes boiled, or dried in the sun or wind, but often raw; for in his wanderings with the people, he had to share their coarse and dirty fare. Anxious for the temporal as well as spiritual benefit of the colony, Egede determined to make the trial of sowing some corn. Accordingly, he caused the long grass to be set on fire, in order to thaw the frozen earth, and then he carefully put in the precious seed. It grew very well till it was in ear; but in September he had to cut it down while it was still unripe, owing to the severe night frosts.

In 1728, his Majesty, Frederick IV., took upon himself to adopt measures for extending the mission, and establishing a settled trade with Greenland. With this view, he sent out several ships, one of which was an armed vessel, with materials to erect a fort, and a small garrison of soldiers to protect the colony. Major Paars was appointed Governor, and Captain Landorp, Commandant. Some more missionaries were also sent. But just as the new colony of Godhaab, or Good Hope, was established, a sickness broke out, and forty people died. To add to their distress, tidings reached them that their noble friend and patron was no more. Frederick IV. was dead; and his successor, Christian VI., sent out an order, in 1731, that the colony should be abandoned, and the settlers should all return home. Egede, in consideration of his long service, was allowed to stay, and to retain any of the colonists who were willing to remain with him. Provision for one year was also given him, but he was expressly told that he must expect no further assistance from Government.

Some of the Greenlanders having been informed, as a reason for the recall, that the King had heard they were little the better for all the instruction they had received, and that they would not seek after God, but still followed their old courses, alleged that whoever had said so to his Majesty had not spoken the truth; and they entreated Egede to remain, and to write and tell the King what a well-behaved people they were.

His heart was heavy at the thought of abandoning his work, and the 150 children whom he had baptized, and was instructing. After much prayer and consideration, he and his noble wife resolved to remain.

The next few years were passed in alternations of hope and fear. In consequence of Egede's urgent representations, notwithstanding his previous refusal, the new King, Christian VI., was pleased to send out a ship with supplies; and soon after he ordered the sum of 2,000 rix-dollars to be given for the support of the mission. The heart of Egede was further cheered by the arrival of three Moravian missionaries. This event opened a new chapter in the history of the Greenland Mission.

CHAPTER XV.

MATTHEW AND CHRISTIAN STACH.

"In due season ye shall reap if ye faint not."

> "Blessed Cross, the symbol thou,
> Once of shame,—of glory now!
> Hallowed banner, wave unfurled,
> Till a ransomed blood-bought world
> Shelter in His bleeding side,
> Bow before the Crucified!"
>
> J. E.

WHILST Egede was working and waiting in Greenland, helpers were being raised up at home. Amongst the noblemen who visited Copenhagen to be present at the coronation of Christian VI., was Count Zinzendorf. While at the capital, he met with two Greenlanders, who had been instructed by Hans Egede, and from them he had the sad tidings that orders were given for the mission to be abandoned.

At this very time it pleased God to put into the hearts of Matthew Stach and Frederick Böhnisch, two simple-minded men, members of the congregation at Herrnhut, an earnest desire to go and preach Christ to the Greenlanders. In that day Copenhagen was the city to which all interested in the work of Christianising the heathen seemed naturally to resort. Accordingly, Stach and Böhnisch at once proceeded thither.*

Matthew Stach, in his own simple narrative, says, "When I first heard of Greenland, I felt a strong desire to go there. My brother and myself did not trouble our heads how we should live there. We hoped that the Apostle of Greenland, Egede, could and would make use of us." On reaching Copenhagen they met with nothing but discouragement. It was urged, that if the learned Egede effected so little, it could not be expected that success would attend the labours of such illiterate men as they were. There was, however, one nobleman at the Court, who seemed better acquainted with the Bible, and God's mode of working, than the rest. Count Von Pless, the King's chamberlain, requested an audience of his Majesty, and reminded him that God had in all ages made use of weak and feeble agents for accomplishing his designs in the world. Professor Ewald, and the Rev. Mr. Reuss, his Majesty's chaplain, also showed them much kindness, although every one around was ridiculing their scheme as wild and

* Böhnisch being on a journey of some length at the time when leave was given for the commencement of the mission, Christian Stach, a cousin of Matthew, was found willing to take his place. Christian David, the well-known Moravian Evangelist, consenting to accompany them, and assist in the establishment of the work.

visionary. In consequence of these representations, the King was so moved, that following the example of his royal predecessor, he promised them assistance, and even wrote a letter to Egede, with his own hand, recommending them to his attention and friendship. The Lord Chamberlain, Von Pless, one day asked them, how they proposed to live in Greenland? "We mean," said they, "to build a house, and to cultivate the land, that we may not be burdensome to any." To this he objected, that there was no wood in the country to build with. "Then," said they, "we will dig into the earth, and lodge there." Struck with their self-denial, he replied, "No! you shall not do that. Take timber with you, and build a house. Accept of these fifty dollars for that purpose."

Not content with helping them himself, Count Von Pless introduced them to several persons of rank, who liberally contributed towards their expenses. With these donations they purchased poles, planks, laths, tools for agriculture and masonry, and implements for fishing and hunting.

To the eye of man there was nothing worthy of note in the humble individuals, who, on that 10th of April, 1733, embarked on board the King's ship, "Caritas," Captain Hildebrand; but in the eye of Heaven that event was doubtless viewed with the deepest interest, and in the last Great Day thousands will join in blessing God, that that mission was founded, and the work undertaken which was that day commenced. After a speedy voyage, they landed safely in Greenland, where they experienced a cordial welcome from Egede.

For some years the brethren at Herrnhut had annually compiled a collection of texts and verses, one for each day in the year. This text was called the "Daily Word." By a remarkable coincidence, the one for the 10th of April, the day on which they sailed, was,—

"Now Faith is the substance of things hoped for,
The evidence of things *not seen*."

"*We* view *Him* whom no eye can see,
With Faith's keen vision steadfastly."

One of Matthew Stach's first letters home contains these words:—"I address you, dear brethren, from a country where the name of Jesus is not yet known, and where the Sun of Righteousness has not yet risen. You live in the bright noon day. The sun has risen upon you. Has he not warmed your hearts; or, are some of you still frozen? The light shines on all of you; but for him who has not yet arisen to walk in the light, it were better to have lived in Greenland, and never to have heard of Jesus. Remember your meanest brother constantly in your prayers."

At times the missionaries were almost overwhelmed by the loneliness of their position. Close fellowship with their Master could alone have sustained them in the long days of apparently hopeless toil in that ice-bound region.

The circumstances in which they found Egede were anything but encouraging. The natives openly mocked and ridiculed him whenever he spoke to them of spiritual things, and often beat their noisiest instruments to drown his voice, and to prevent hearing his words of warning. In 1735 a terrible calamity overtook them, and famine, with all its horrors, seemed inevitable. The natives no sooner learnt that they were in want, than they raised the price of all provisions. The season was a bad one, both for fishing and hunting, and the annual supply from home had not arrived. The missionaries often had nothing to eat but the remnant of their oatmeal, mixed with train oil; though this was, they said, a delicacy, compared to the old tallow candles to which they were afterwards reduced. Once, after subsisting for several days on shell-fish and seaweed, a boatman found a dead whale, and gave them a meal of it. Another time, having eaten only shell-fish for five days, they were so weak, that on returning from a fruitless fishing expedition, their united strength was unequal to draw the boat up to land. In this emergency a native came from a distance, bringing them a porpoise, of which they all thankfully partook. Once, after an unsuccessful day's chase, they were driven upon a desert island, and, when almost starving, an eagle flew over their head, which one of the party immediately shot. It afforded them several meals, and also supplied them with quills for writing, of which they stood in great need. In 1734 the ranks of the missionaries were reinforced by the arrival of a fresh party of Brethren, which enabled them the more readily to dispense with the services of Christian David and Christian Stach, the former of whom returned to Europe in the autumn of 1735, the latter in 1736. A few years later another missionary returned home, taking with him two native Greenlanders. One of these died on the voyage, but the other, on his return, gave his countrymen a far clearer notion of Denmark, and of the habits and customs of civilised life, than they had ever had before.

His account of the Danish Royal Family, to whom he had the honour of being presented, and of the Court, the stately churches and public buildings, and, above all, an exhibition of the many presents he brought back, excited the greatest surprise, and created a desire in the heart of many a Greenlander to visit the grand country, and behold its wonders.

The visit of this native tended much, indirectly, to raise the missionaries in the estimation of his people. The lad's description of the military power and splendour of the King awakened novel reflections amongst men who had hitherto been accustomed to associate wealth and greatness with the man who could catch most seals. The Greenlanders were especially struck with the fact, which seems deeply to have impressed the young traveller, that this Danish monarch, with all his grandeur, sat meekly to hear God's Word preached by his own subjects, and that he knelt low at the feet of Him whom he acknowledged to be "King of kings, and Lord of lords."

The newly arrived Moravian missionaries found Egede suffering from a combination of trials. The natives mocked and insulted him whenever he spoke of spiritual things. The commencement of their missionary career was marked with trials of no common kind. Their goods were stolen, and they themselves laid prostrate with small-pox, caught in nursing the sick natives. The difficulties which these unlettered men had to encounter in acquiring the language, would have proved absolutely insurmountable, had they not been endowed with an extraordinary measure of patience. They had to learn Danish before they could even understand their instructors; and as they had probably never seen a grammar, it must have been no easy task for them even to form distinct ideas of the numerous terms employed in the intricate science of language. After this they had to acquire the Greenland language, and to commit to memory a large vocabulary of words. The savages around them aggravated all their other difficulties by stealing the books they had written with immense labour and care.*

As yet they had not been cheered by one single conversion. Night after night they assembled after the toils of the day, to commune with each other, and their God. "It must have been a strange scene," says their biographer, Crantz, "in the thick gloom of a Greenland evening, when their solitary lamp dimly lighted the chamber, and these five men rose alternately and told of their struggles and sadness." The doors and walls were plastered over with frost; the beds were frozen to the bedstead; the linen frozen in the drawers; the barrels had to be hewn in pieces to get out the meat; and when thawed in snow-water, and set on the fire, the outside was boiled before the inside could be pierced with a knife.

* See Crantz's History, and Brown's History.

One day when hope had sunk low, the subject of their return home was brought forward; but Matthew Stach said he could not *think even* of leaving; and he quoted his favourite verse: "At evening time it shall be light." And, ere long, the light began to shine.

The brethren are again assembled; a few natives are gathered round them. The New Testament is opened, and one of their number, John Beck, reads aloud. . The chapter chosen is the account of the Saviour's agony in Gethsemane. As the words fell on their ears, God opened the heart of one of them. Kayarnak rose up, stood in front of the speaker, and said with a loud and earnest voice, " How was that ? Tell me that once more, for I, too, would fain be saved."

These words kindled the whole soul of the missionary into ardour. He again gave the account of the Saviour's sufferings and death; and soon many of the Greenlanders began to pray. Shortly after, Kayarnak and his family were baptized. His heart was so full of happiness, that he began to tell his heathen countrymen around him about Jesus. Being invited by some natives to join in a dance at the sun feast, he refused, saying, " I have now another kind of joy. Christ has arisen in my heart." Nothing that the missionaries said impressed these people so much as witnessing the change in their own relatives and friends. Their lives were so different to what they had formerly been. And when the converts prayed they were still more astonished. They thought, at first, that the prayers were committed to memory, and wanted to learn them also; but they were told that they must first feel their own want and misery, and then a sense of need would teach them how to pray. The converts were now of great use in helping the missionaries, not only in speaking to others, but in translating the Gospels into the Greenland language. In a few years they translated the whole of the New Testament, besides many parts of the Old Testament, a spelling book and hymn book; and, before they left the work to their successors, they completed, with great pains, a grammar and dictionary in this barbarous language.

From this era may be dated a new and improved disposition amongst the natives towards their instructors, though many continued very untractable. Some who had ill-treated the missionaries now made voyages to come and ask their pardon; and amongst those who had been their greatest opposers, there were men who would stand watching along the shore, as they sailed by, *entreating them to land*, and tell them the words of God.*

* Crantz's "History of Greenland," vol. ii. pp. 34, 38.

Some time after, the missionaries had the great delight of saving the lives of fifty unfortunate Europeans. Their ships, thirty in number, were blocked up by the ice and fourteen of them were shattered to pieces. Many of the crew died of cold and hunger, but others had strength enough to travel over the ice to land. Twelve were found by some Christian Greenlanders on a desert island, more dead than alive. All these unfortunate people were welcomed as brethren, fed and clothed, and then sent forward to the Danish colonies, from whence they ultimately obtained a passage to Europe.

Surely these men, on their return, would speak well of missionaries and their converts! Had the same event happened some years earlier, they would doubtless have been robbed and murdered by the very men who now, having learned the love of Christ, desired themselves to minister to the wants of these strangers.

The King of Denmark having made known his wish, that more missionaries might be sent, the brethren determined to add two to their number. For this purpose Frederick Böhnisch, who at the first had volunteered to go, but who had been destined for the mission to St. Thomas's, was now selected, and John Beck accompanied him. Both of these men proved devoted labourers. When at Copenhagen, they drew up a memorial which was presented to the King through the Baron Von Soelenthal, who had several interviews with the missionaries with reference to their work. Soon after they received the pleasing intelligence, that it was his Majesty's orders that they should have their passage to Greenland free of expense. Mr. Ohnsong, another Danish missionary, sailed at the same time, taking with him Egede's eldest son, who had finished his university studies, and received ordination. But like his father, he gave up all his worldly prospects at home, to tell the Greenlanders of a Saviour's dying love.

CHAPTER XVI.

JOYS AND SORROWS.

"Work while the daylight lasteth,
Ere the shades of night come on,
Ere the Lord of the vineyard cometh
And the labourer's work is done."

STILL through evil and through good report, these devoted servants of God laboured on. The desire to spend their lives amongst the heathen had not been a hasty impulse, and amidst every variety of trial they resolved steadily to pursue this one object. It may well be supposed, that during the long night of toil, since the formation of the mission, these much tried men had experienced almost every variety of trial; but another, of a nature wholly unanticipated, awaited them.

Strong in their faith in God, the members of the mission families had gone in and out, fearlessly amongst the natives, without any apprehension of personal violence. But it happened one day, when the brethren were absent with a number of their followers, that a party of Southland heathens resolved to put in execution a preconcerted plan, and carry off young Anna Stach.

One of their number had seen her, and thinking no Greenland bride worthy of him, determined to take her by force and make her his wife. Seizing the opportunity, when only the women were at home, he paid a visit to the settlement, in company with a party of his friends. Anna was outside the house on their approach. Fortunately, she understood their language, and gathering some notion of their design from an expression she overheard, she hurried back and bolted the door. The ruffians, after some fruitless attempts to burst it open, tried to cut through the windows with their large knives, supposing them to be made of seal blubber, like their own. Their endeavours were unavailing, and by the good providence of God, being unacquainted with the properties of glass, it never occurred to them to dash it in pieces. After some vain efforts, being fearful of the return of the Brethren, they made off, threatening to return. In three days, to Anna's terror, they were again seen approaching in greater numbers, but were happily repulsed by some Greenland friends, aided by a few boatmen from the colony. Soon after Anna was happily married to the missionary, Frederick Böhnisch, and became a most valuable helpmeet in his arduous work, though it is easy to imagine she would never forget the alarm occasioned by her fierce Greenland lover. It was while the mission party were happily assembled to celebrate this marriage, that Kayarnak, the first convert, unexpectedly entered the room, after a year's absence, bringing with him his brother and the whole family. It was indeed a joyful surprise. Many had been the fears of the brethren lest temptation should prove too strong for him, and Kayarnak should be induced to return to his sins and superstitions. But God had kept him, and he had remained faithful. Before leaving the mission-station, he had told them that his object was to make known the good tidings to his relatives, who had never heard of Christ, and though separated from the missionaries, he should not be separated from the missionaries' God. And now, having for a whole year preached the truth to the savages of the South, he said he felt a longing to see the teachers once more. Having left his son behind to read the Scriptures to those who were willing to hear, he joyfully returned to the settlement, which he reached just at the hour when the marriage of Frederick Böhnisch and Anna Stach was being celebrated.

Kayarnak made one more journey to tell his countrymen of Him whom he always spoke of as the "Friend of Sinners." Returning to the station, he was taken ill. He had preached Christ by his life, and now was to proclaim Him by his death. In the midst of acute pain he exhorted, and prayed with such fervour that the Greenlanders were quite amazed. Seeing his children weep, he said, "Don't grieve for me. Have you not heard that believers when they die go to our Saviour, and partake of His eternal joy? You know I was the first amongst us that was converted by Him, and now he calls me first home to Himself." The Danish missionaries visited him daily, as well as the Moravian brethren. Just before he died he told them that all he had heard in the days of health was now made much clearer to his mind. By the desire of his wife and brother, themselves also converts, he was buried with Christian rites; the Danish missionaries giving an exhortation at his grave from the words, "I am the resurrection and the life." In this address he told the astonished heathen, some of whom had never heard the truth before, that a Christian does not die, but at his departure from this world begins truly to live, and will live for evermore. "We then," says the missionary, "kneeled down upon the snow, under the open sky, and gave back to our Saviour this firstling, with our fervent thanks for the grace he had bestowed upon him."

Soon after, a very aged man came to Brother Drachart, asking to be baptized with his two daughters. "It is true," said he, "I can say but little. Thou canst see that my hairs are quite grey, and I am very old, but I believe with all my heart in Jesus Christ." One of the expressive sayings of the baptized was, "I am determined to become the Saviour's property."

For the first time this year, 1741, the two congregations of the Danish and Moravian Missionaries united in the festive commemoration of Christmas, with their once heathen converts. "From this time," they say, "we thought it would be more conducive to the welfare of the flock to notice more particularly the general feasts of the Church." Three Greenlanders were baptized, when hymns were sung in Greenlandish, German, and Danish, as most of the sailors from the colony were present. On partaking of the Holy Communion the joy of some of the converts was so great, that tears rolled down their cheeks abundantly. They spoke afterwards of that season, as "closest fellowship with Christ," and one said, "Our only thought was, how is it possible that the Saviour can love us poor men so exceedingly."

The next event was the death of Barzillai, the oldest man in the settlement. He was a very intelligent person, and much respected. One of his heathen countrymen visiting him, said, "Hast thou seen the God of whom thou speakest so?"

He replied, "I have not seen Him, but I love Him with my whole heart; and I, and all true believers, will soon see Him with our bodily eyes." In the winter of 1757, the converts gave an edifying proof that they possessed the faith which "worketh by love." As heathens, they were cruel and hard-hearted to their own nearest relatives. As Christians, they "honoured all men," and "sought not their own." A letter from Denmark came to the missionaries, giving an account of the destruction of an Indian settlement, in Pennsylvania, by a party of savages. It told how those, who had escaped the general massacre, went to the Mission-station, and were hospitably received. No sooner had these once cruel Greenlanders heard these tidings, than they burst into loud weeping, and were eager to contribute to the relief of these unknown brethren. One said, "I have a fine reindeer skin, which I will give." "I," said another, "have a pair of reindeer boots, which I will send." "I," added a third, "will send a seal, and then they will have something to eat and to burn." Surely such a fact is a living commentary on the power of true religion, to ennoble and expand the most ferocious hearts.

Six more converts died happily this year. One young woman, Susanna, said, on her death-bed, "Oh, how glad I am, that I have a Saviour!

If I could not rely upon Him, I should be afraid of death." One of the great difficulties of the missionaries was, to find food for the aged and orphans, who constantly flocked to them, on being deserted by their heathen relatives. They had long made it a rule that one of their number should accompany their flock on their fishing expeditions, and should catch fish himself, to have a supply for the needy, as well as to watch over and teach his people. A yearly list was sent to Copenhagen of the articles of food required, in which all fared alike. No one thought himself above manual labour; and whatever one had was shared by all. In 1764, there were many changes, owing to deaths and removals. Our old friend, Matthew Stach took a long voyage south, to investigate the state of the country and its inhabitants. Unlike many travellers, the Brethren have very few 'wonders' to narrate. Indeed, the very quiet way in which they tell of hair-breadth escapes, and marvellous incidents, almost provokes a smile. Thus, in his journey south, to which allusion has been made, Stach quaintly tells, that he, with his native helper, Rudberg, was overtaken by a storm. He says, "Rudberg, being provided with snow shoes, was only driven like a ship under sail to the nearest settlement, whilst for myself, the wind causing me to approach too near the brink of a precipice, I fell headlong into the valley below, but fortunately pitching into a snow-drift. escaped unhurt, and so went on my way."

Narratives like this abound in the journals of these simple-hearted men.

It has been said, and we think with truth, that one reason why the whole Christian world has not been startled by the recital of their labours, is, that the tale has been told with such singular humility as scarcely to enable people to realise the facts, or to form even a faint idea of the amount of hardship undergone. Truly, " as good soldiers of Jesus Christ," have these beloved brethren " endured hardness." Of them, as of Moses, the Servant of God, it may well be said that, they " had respect unto the recompense of the reward," and " endured as seeing Him who is invisible."

Some time, in the year following, 1767, we find, by Stach's journal, that he returned in safety to his own station. There, intelligence had just arrived, by the ship yearly sent out, of the death of Frederick the Fifth, and the accession of Christian the Seventh, to the throne of Denmark.

The Greenlanders were assembled for the notification of the mournful event, reminded of all the blessings they had enjoyed under the benign government of the deceased monarch, and informed of the request of his successor to be remembered in their prayers. Would that such prayers were asked for in our own days! All present then fell upon their knees, and the missionary implored the continuance of the Divine blessing on that Royal house, which had set such a bright example to all other European potentates, in being the first to encourage and support the endeavours of pious Christians, to rescue their heathen subjects from the chains of darkness. At the close of every sentence, the congregation responded— "Hear us, gracious Lord and God!" Several natives from Kookoernen now embraced Christianity, and whole families removed to live near the station. Some came as the result of Stach's journey; others from hearing the Gospel through Tokko, who had placed himself under the care of Mr. Brasen, a young Danish surgeon, at New Herrnhutt, and had thus been led to embrace the truth. Thirty persons were in this way added to the congregation.

In the journals of these good men, it is incidentally mentioned, that while the numbers to be taught increased, the teachers were for a time partially unfitted for their duties.

The cause is thus simply stated. Owing to the great scarcity of drift-wood for firing, in that rough climate, they were compelled to seek a substitute in the bushes at the farthest extremity of the bay. The sun having more power there than on the open sea-coast, they grow to a larger size. The collecting of these bushes was, however, attended with both trouble and danger; for it was necessary to carry them down the almost perpendicular edges of rocks, which fence the shore, and then to cut them into small pieces, as their crooked shape would otherwise have made it impossible to get sufficient into the boat. This labour was rendered more harassing by innumerable swarms of flies, which had established themselves among the bushes, and defended their possessions with such vigour, that the eyes of the missionaries were quite swollen up with the inflammation produced by the bites.

Some of them suffered so severely, as for a time to be seriously hindered in their work.

In 1794, two of the missionaries having to explore a neighbouring island for drift-wood, were completely surrounded by ice, and confined in that dreary spot for upwards of a fortnight. Several attempts were made to reach them with food, but the kayaks found it impossible to penetrate the ice. The missionaries thankfully record that they caught fish enough to preserve life, and at length made their way through the ice, at great risk, to the main land, where they had to undertake a long journey over steep hills, and at last reached home, having been absent a whole month.

Thus simply is recorded the reason why, for that month, additional labour devolved upon the brethren left in charge of the converts.

Volumes might be written of the hardships and casualties to which life is subject in these arctic regions.

One of the missionaries, named Grillich, left Greenland for Europe in October, 1798, on business connected with the Mission. After drifting about for five weeks, the vessel was so much damaged by the drift-ice that she was obliged to return. On its being refitted, he again embarked in the same ship, but the quantity of drift-ice was greater than before. At length the captain, finding the ship so clogged and damaged that he could not hope to save her, resolved to quit her with all the property on board. The whole ship's company began their march back, over the ice, dragging the boat after them. Thus two nights were spent in the open air with no sustenance but that afforded by drinking the melted snow. On the third day they came to open water, when they launched their boat, and once more reached the barren coast of Greenland. Scarcely had they landed, when a tremendous storm arose, with snow and sleet, and thus the night was spent, without either food or covering. After a further detention of a month they once more embarked, and finally arrived at Copenhagen towards the close of the following year.

When war with England broke out, in 1807, their troubles were fearfully increased, as the regular annual supply from Denmark was interrupted. This roused them to the recollection of their dependent and precarious situation, especially as it affected their wives and children. They were often without the actual necessaries of life; their store of clothes was nearly exhausted, and they had no tobacco. This article, being the current coin of the country, was essential for purposes of barter. Their stock of wine was so reduced that they could rarely celebrate the Holy Communion, which caused them much grief.

The Danish Government sent express orders that the Mission settlements should have a proportionate share of the provisions sent to these colonies; but it fell far short of their wants. Many of the inhabitants of those inhospitable shores were driven to support life by eating muscles and seaweed.

In this distressed condition they continued till

1811, when the British Government generously afforded the Danes every facility for supplying their Greenland colonies, by permitting all Danish vessels, furnished with a proper license, to sail thither. The missionary, Henry Meutzel, who had passed thirty-three years of his life in active service, was at this time taken to his rest.

British Christians, living in comfort and luxury at home, can scarcely form an idea of the amount of self-denial involved in the patient toil of a life of thirty-three years on this iron-bound soil. The labourers in this part of the mission field were not excited by temporary enthusiasm; but, animated by a deep-seated love of souls, they plodded on, through evil and through good report, in humble imitation of Him who pleased not Himself, and left his children an example that they should walk in his steps. A striking instance of self-denial was exhibited in the commencement of the mission to the South Greenlanders. When the Settlement of Lichtenfels was founded, in 1758, Matthew Stach could not be happy, he said, without trying to win over some of these benighted savages to the Saviour. Mention has been already made of this journey, but a detailed account of it would fill a volume. After many perils, he reached Fisher's Bay, accompanied by the faithful brethren Jans and Peter Haven.

The factor at Zukkertop gave them a hearty welcome, and urged their settling near him. But, adhering to their old rule, they resolved to fix their head-quarters where the greatest number of natives was likely to be found. Accordingly, they began to rear their little home of stones at Akonemiok, not deterred by the dread of starvation, and though it was so situated that they could never catch a ray of the sun, owing to a screen of lofty mountains. The natives did not want them, and would render no help in the building of their hut. They were forced themselves to roll every stone to the spot, to carry the earth in bags, and to fetch the sods by water, from a distant spot. This house, when built, consisted of a room five yards square, and a small kitchen. The roof was covered with a double layer of sods, cemented with earth, and spread over with old tent skins. God's blessing rested upon their efforts, and in little more than a year twenty-two natives had avouched themselves to be the Lord's children. Soon after several of them were called home. They died happy in Jesus. One exclaimed, with her dying breath, "I have no other joy but in my Saviour alone! He loves me! My body is decayed by sickness, but I rejoice exceedingly in the prospect of the blessed moment when my Saviour will call me. I am redeemed with His precious blood. I love Him, and shall love Him for ever. My greatest desire is to be with Him!" And with these, and similar words on her lips, poor Judith, the once savage Greenlander, fell asleep.

In one of the late festival commemorations of the Brethren's Missions, the Greenland congregations held special services, in order to unite with their friends all over the world in devout praise and thankfulness to God for his grace, power, and faithfulness displayed towards one of the smallest and feeblest of churches.

The Danish Mission to Greenland continues under the direction of the State, as it has been since the time of Hans Egede. The anniversary missionary meeting was held this year at Ribe, a town in the Duchy of Schleswig, when a large number of the friends of missions assembled from all parts of the country. Dr. Kalkar, the President of the Society, then presented a Report on the State of Christianity in Greenland. He announced that the translation of the Bible into the Greenlandish language had been revised with much care, and that a new edition was shortly to appear. He spoke of the blessing which had attended the work in that country, and which was proved by the entrance of Greenlanders into the

Society, as missionaries to their fellow countrymen. At the close, an address was drawn up, in which it was urged that the Church in Denmark should take more interest than it has hitherto done in missionary labours. Dr. Roerdam, the Head of the Mission College, reported that there were at present five young men studying in order to be qualified for missionary work.

We cannot better conclude this simple narrative than by making some extracts from the letters of two converted Greenlanders to Bishop Johannes De Watteville, who had paid an official visit to the Mission, in the year 1752. The Christian reader will enjoy the artless expression of their feelings, and many will regard them in the light of a literary curiosity:—

"My dear Johannes, full of love!

"How much thou didst love me, when here, I cannot forget, because thou gavest food to my soul.

"When thou, concerning the Saviour's death and wounds, didst often instruct me, these thy words did pervade my heart in such a manner that since that time I nothing besides can relish. No other thing can rejoice me but the Redeemer's death. For my poor heart I nothing else will have; this suffices me entirely.

"That in company with thy and my beloved

Beck I came to 'this place thou knowest already; and since, according to the will of the Saviour, it was so to be, he gives me words to the baptized ones, and likewise to the heathen. I will acquaint thee what words I make use of; 'tis in this manner:—

"'Formerly I was just as you are, an ignorant and wicked man, and to this hour I have, in my inner parts, nothing good of myself. But the Redeemer has sought and found me; and by His word called me; and from the heathen set me free; and to the congregation of the faithful brought me. And when I was yet a miserable man, He, by His Spirit, instructed me; and through His blood washed away my sins.

"'But wherewith hath He redeemed me? With His own blood inestimable, and with His innocent sufferings and death. Hark ye! so exceedingly has the Saviour loved mankind, in order that they might become his property, if your hearts to Him *now* you will surrender, then He will Himself prepare them and make you happy.' Thus I used to speak to them. Thou knowest also that when thou wast here, I obtained an helpmate by God's will.

"Before His eyes we both live contented, and the love of us both towards Him increases. Towards each other we are friendly; and all that we have to transact, we do it before our Saviour's eyes.

"It is, indeed, agreeable, when married people together before our Saviour live happily, and prove a help to one another in all things. I, that live at Lichtenfels,—A. K."

Another old couple wrote as follows :—

"We are happy. Our Saviour has made us to be of one mind, and He has also warmed our hearts. Now our constant prayer is, that they may never grow cold again. By His blood He can preserve them burning.

"We give you thanks that you have sent us a house, in which we can daily hear of our dear Saviour and hold our meetings. Although we are very deficient, yet we feel that the Saviour often melts our hearts as the sun melts the snow; and then it is as with the lamp when fresh oil is poured into it; it burns brighter, and can enkindle others. If we be with heathens, we tell them that our Saviour has redeemed them also with His blood; and that if they would believe in Him, they might be as happy as we and the other believers are. In this manner we discourse to our countrymen; for since we have learned to know our Saviour in this light, we love Him with our whole hearts, and rejoice in Him."

God grant that the words of these poor Greenlanders may prove a blessing to some enlightened reader in civilized Britain, who has never yet experienced the Saviour's love in his heart as a personal reality."

Before concluding this record of toil and self-denial, a word must be said about the labourers now in the field. These devoted men are pursuing their work with the same ardour as their predecessors. Mr. Kögel's increasing years and infirmities making it needful for him to return to Europe, he writes, "The thoughts of my approaching separation from this people, after a residence among them of thirty-six years, is very painful." He then mentions, that the last winter has been a very trying one, owing to storms, which prevented the Greenlanders securing a needed supply of food; and that no rain having fallen for nearly three months, they were suffering greatly from drought.

As might be expected, the missionaries were all deeply interested in the result of Colonel Shaffner's attempt to effect a telegraphic communication between Europe and America by way of Greenland. Should it prove successful, it would, indeed, be a boon to our friends in that ice-bound region, as at present, they only hear from the rest of the world once during each year.

CHAPTER XVII.

WEST INDIA ISLANDS.

"To them that have no might, He increaseth strength."

"Since Jesus will employ thee, wake
Each noble energy ;
For all *He* bids thee undertake,
His might shall strengthen thee."

How various are the ways in which God works, and how different the kinds of agency which He is pleased to employ! This is strikingly illustrated in the history of the introduction of Christianity into the West India Islands. A little captive maid was the honoured instrument of leading Naaman to the wonder-working prophet, who not only healed his body, but made known to his guilty soul the God of Israel. In like manner, a negro slave, taken by his master to Copenhagen, was the instrument of stirring up Christian hearts to pity, and to make efforts on behalf of his oppressed countrymen.

We have seen in the preceding chapters, how zealously the Danish King and his Government set themselves to propagate Christianity in Greenland and the East.

But there were other possessions belonging to Denmark, and it is to them we would now introduce our readers. The islands of St. Thomas, Saint Croix, St. Jan, and St. Peter, in the West Indies, were dependencies of that crown.

The inhabitants, whether slaves, or free men, were living without any knowledge of God. Their situation was touchingly described by a negro servant, named Anthony, who had been brought by his owner to Copenhagen a short time before the coronation of King Christian VI. He there became acquainted with some of the followers of Count Zinzendorf, that nobleman having left his home in Saxony, to be present on the occasion.

Anthony's story was repeated by his servants to the Count; and ere long it came to the ears of the Moravian Church, at Herrnhutt, in Upper Lusatia. Two of its number were so moved with pity, that they resolved to embark for the West Indies, and devote themselves to the instruction of some of the wretched slaves.

The first step was to make their way to Copenhagen. There they felt sure of meeting with Christian kindness and judicious advice. On their way they visited a number of friends, the majority of whom tried to dissuade them from their design, representing the difficulties and dangers with which it would be attended.

14*

Some, however, took an opposite view. Amongst these was the Countess of Stollberg, who encouraged them much, saying, "That every Christian should account it an honour to die, if required, for his Master's cause." Count Zinzendorf also took the same view. Arrived at Copenhagen, their difficulties seemed only to increase.

They were told that no ship would take them to St. Thomas; and that should they even get there, it was extremely doubtful whether they would find it possible to preach to the negroes. Nothing daunted, these two noble men declared that they were quite willing to be themselves *sold as slaves*, in order that by that means they might obtain access to the negroes as *fellow-workers*, and so make known to them the truths of the Gospel.

At Copenhagen they first heard, that the idea of selling themselves as slaves was quite out of the question, as no white man could be employed in that capacity. Notwithstanding these disappointments, Leonard Dober and David Nitschman remained firm to their purpose. The less help they experienced from man, the more they looked to God.

Struck with their steadfastness, several influential persons began to view their design with a favourable eye. Amongst these were his Majesty's two chaplains and several counsellors of state. Ultimately, some members of the royal family promised that they would befriend and assist them.*

With this help their slender outfit was soon prepared, their passage taken, and on the 13th of December, 1732, after a voyage of ten weeks, they landed at St. Thomas. On leaving, one of their noble patrons parted from them with these words, "Go, in God's name. Our Saviour chose fishermen to preach His Gospel; and He Himself was a carpenter, and the son of a carpenter." One Danish friend, unknown to the missionaries, wrote to an honest man at St. Thomas's, who gave them a home in his house for the first few days after their arrival. Nitschman found sufficient employment as a carpenter to enable him to keep himself, and Dober attempted to work at his trade as a potter, both being unwilling to depend upon others for their maintenance. This source failing him, he earned a scanty living by keeping watch on the plantations, and other services.

For some time Nitschman gave him all the help in his power; but circumstances obliged him to return to Europe, and then poor Dober was, indeed, destitute. For many weeks he subsisted chiefly on bread and water. But under all diffi-

* "Oldendorp's Geschichte," tom. ii., p. 456.

culties, his missionary zeal seems never in the least to have abated. The complete isolation, experienced by Dober and other early missionaries, was, perhaps, the greatest trial amongst the many by which they were surrounded. At times he felt it well-nigh insupportable. But he was not forgotten by the Church at home; and before two years had passed, fellow-helpers arrived.

Every day's residence in the Danish Islands convinced the missionaries that the half had not been told them, of the sin and wretchedness of their inhabitants.

No pen can describe the awful state of degradation in which the slaves were sunk.

Dark and magical rites, incantations, and barbarous customs were continually practised.

Obeahism and Fetishism prevailed, accompanied by all the terrors that the dread of an unknown malignant Being, supposed to be ever near, could inspire.

To such an extent did Obeahism prevail, and so often did it cause the death of its victims, that at length it became a crime punishable with death by slave-law. One missionary says,—" Obeahism and Fetishism constituted a mystery of iniquity never fully revealed to the uninitiated. The oath was taken under a pledge of inviolable secresy, and was usually administered previously to insurrections, or individual murders. Blood was drawn from each individual present: this was mixed with grave-earth and gunpowder in a bowl, and then all present partook of it.

Moral honesty, and a regard for truth, were unknown. The negroes were utterly unable to distinguish between truth and falsehood. In negro parlance, "truth" was designated "telling lies to buckra." Hence, it was most difficult for the missionaries to obtain a correct answer from a negro on the most trifling subjects.

Their ideas of theft were similar to their views of falsehood. To steal from an owner, was thought perfectly justifiable; it was only a *crime* when committed against each other. The following anecdote will illustrate this: "Me don't tief nothing," maintained a negro, who was caught by the overseer in the very act of stealing sugar. Again and again the slave protested that he was innocent. "What do you mean?" said the newly-arrived overseer, not yet acquainted with negro rules of morality, "Haven't you got the stolen sugar now in your possession?"

"Yes; but me don't tief it; me only take it, massa." "What do you mean by that?" "Why, as sugar belongs to massa, and myself belongs to massa, it all de same ting, dat make me tell massa me don't tief it; me only take it." "What do you call thieving then," said the astonished overseer, when convinced the man was really in earnest. "When me broke into my broder's house, and take away his tings, den me tief, massa."

As an escape from the miseries of slavery, suicide was awfully prevalent. At one period, this crime was committed to such an extent, that the legislature passed a law, that every one guilty of it, should be hung in chains on the public roads, till devoured by birds of prey.

Volumes might be filled with a description of the scenes of sin and misery which our missionaries met with on their arrival. Unused to a kind word or a kind look, the negroes regarded every friendly overture with suspicion. Other labourers had *their* difficulties, and they were many; but the *first* pioneers had every barrier to break down, and not one outward comfort to sustain them.

So universal was the profligacy, that a planter, who himself made no profession of religion, addressed one of the missionaries with these words: "This island is a hell upon earth." Around all was misery and sin; the missionaries themselves were poor, sick, and friendless; there was but one bright spot, and to that they were ever looking —it was Heaven.*

* Philippo's "Past and Present of Jamaica."

It was their hope in Heaven which alone sustained the hearts of these Christian heroes. The social condition of the slaves was deplorable. That of their white masters was, morally, but little better. Unsoftened by domestic ties, without hope, and without God in the world, whether the missionary entered the spacious dwelling of the master, or the squalid hovel of the slave, he found alike in both—" hatred, variance, wrath, strife, and revelling."

The indolence of the negro, under the deadening influence of slavery, has ever been proverbial, and the missionary found himself called upon on the one hand, to remonstrate with the owner for his fearful cruelty, and with the negro for his determined idleness.

Without hope, both for this world and the next, was it likely that the poor oppressed slave should work one moment longer than he was driven, by the stimulus of the lash?

Into the cruelties practised upon them, it is not our purpose here to enter. Reference is only made to the subject to enable the reader more fully to comprehend the difficulties which beset our friends, on commencing their work.

It is hardly possible in this day, with the widest stretch of imagination, to form any idea of the vice and ignorance with which they had to contend.

The entire ignorance of the natives, in a land where the Bible had never been seen, nor a school heard of; where the art of computation by figures was unknown; and the only belief was, a conviction that black men were prohibited all knowledge, by a decree of the Almighty; it is hard in the present day to bring the mind to realize.

The current tradition was, that at the creation of the world, there was both a *white* and *black* progenitor.

That to try their dispositions the Almighty let down two boxes from heaven, of unequal dimensions, of which the black man had the first choice. Influenced by his propensity to greediness, he chose the largest, and the smaller one consequently fell to the share of the white. "Buckra-box," the blacks say, was "full up with pen, paper, and whip," and "negro-box," with "hoe and bill, bill and hoe."

Their oppressors of that day, frequently wrote of the blacks as a race incapable of acquiring knowledge, a connecting link between the animal and intellectual economies; affiliated to the ourangoutang, and like that animal, actuated by instinct, not reason. They were said to be unable to compare, to argue, or to combine ideas. Long, a West Indian planter and historian says—"A black is unable to place a table square in a room, from a defect of vision similar to that of the ourang-outang." Hume, in his observations on the native Africans, says,—"They are inferior to the rest of the species, and utterly incapable of the higher attainments of the mind." Montesquieu says, "They are not human beings, but occupy an intermediate rank, below the whites, and are destined by the Creator to be the slaves of their superiors."

It was amongst a people thus sunk and degraded that Dober and Nitschman took up their abode. If ever the power of the Gospel was tested it surely was it this case, and well has it stood the test.

The relatives of Anthony were the earliest converts, and ere the missionaries had been five years engaged in their self-denying work, they numbered their disciples by hundreds. Death and disease, it is true, had been amongst them; and as one party after another arrived to sustain the Mission, they fell victims to the insalubrity of the climate. Still there was never wanting a band of volunteers to come forward to be baptized for the dead, and thus reinforce their diminished ranks.

Their faith and patience had been tried in various ways. Truly did they carry about with them the marks of their apostleship. Like St. Paul, they had been, " in journeyings oft, in perils of waters, in perils of robbers, in perils by their own countrymen, in perils by the heathen, in perils in the city, in perils in the wilderness, in perils on the sea, in weariness and painfulness, in watchings often, in hunger and thirst, in fastings often, in cold and nakedness, besides that which came upon them daily, the care of all the churches."

One day a master met an old negro woman, who had been a favourite household servant. She had recently joined the band of converts.

"If you had not gone to those enthusiasts," said he, "you should have had a good provision in your old age; but now, unless you leave those people your present allowance will be stopped."

"Me quite sorry," was the answer, "that massa angry with him old servant so, but if massa vex because me take up God's work, well den me can't help it; begging massa's pardon, God's anger worser than massa's, and me soul wants more feed than me body does. God promise, me no want no good ting: and massa Jesus say, 'What profit a man to have the whole world and lose him own soul.'"

Many instances occurred in which freedom was offered to Christian slaves on condition of their leaving off praying. One is given as a specimen.

A negro woman with six children, had on

account of her devoted attendance upon some part of her master's family, been promised her freedom. The manumission papers for herself and her children were actually prepared.

She had heard of the missionaries, and lately had attended their meetings. Her master sent for her, and asked her if it was true. She simply said she had begun to pray. He then told her, unless she would at once give up hearing the missionaries, she should not have her liberty. She wept bitterly. He argued with her, but she said her mind was made up. She could not sin against God. Her master then gave her a few days to consider. At the end of the time, he sent for her again. The papers were shown her, and the terms once more proposed. As the tears coursed down her sable cheeks, she faltered out, with an almost bursting heart, "Massa, me want to be free, but me cannot deny me Saviour." The enraged owner ordered her to take the papers, and burn them in the fire. She did so, and stood by till they were consumed to ashes.

Some considerable time after, the wife of one of the missionaries had the delight of procuring the freedom of that poor slave and her children.

A year after Dober's arrival at St. Thomas's, a large party sailed from Europe to recruit the Mission. Thus reinforced, they travelled to every part of the island, preaching the Gospel; and many negroes began to inquire what they must do to be saved.

This aroused much enmity; and Satan, unwilling to lose his prey, stirred up a bitter opposition amongst the inhabitants. Some tried to excite the Government to suppress the Mission; others sought to lead the converts into the commission of sin, and thus bring discredit upon the Christian name. To crown all, two of the missionaries, Frederick Martin and his assistant, Freundlich and his wife, were thrown into prison; —one, on a charge of having married a couple, before the validity of his ordination had been ascertained from Denmark; the other, as being privy to a theft.* For these supposed offences, they were imprisoned and fined.

The 1st of January, 1739, found these innocent persons immured in a West Indian prison, with no apparent hope of deliverance. They had proved the "tender mercies" of their enemies to be cruel. Their poverty forbade the hope that they could pay the fine imposed upon them, which amounted to thirty rix dollars; their health was failing under the confinement. They had no hope but in their God. To Him they committed their cause. And He proved Himself "a present help" in this time of trouble.

The same mighty arm that sent an angel out of heaven, to deliver His servant Peter from the prison, where Herod's malice had immured him, sent a messenger of mercy to our captive brethren.

Count Zinzendorf, knowing nothing of the matter, felt it in his heart to go and see how it fared with the brethren at St. Thomas's. He sailed from Copenhagen, accompanied by two missionaries and their wives, and reached St. Thomas's at the end of January, at the very time when all around seemed darkest. On his arrival, the sad story was told to him. He immediately applied to the Governor; the matter was investigated, and the missionaries triumphantly delivered. On the Count's return to Copenhagen, he took back a grateful address to the King of Denmark, from the Christian negroes under the charge of the missionaries, and one to the Queen from the negresses.

During his stay, he frequently addressed large companies of negroes, after their daily labours were finished; and his journals record his surprise and joy at the extent of the field which God had opened for His servants.

But the hostility of their enemies was no way abated. Some insisted that the missionaries should be banished the island; others, that they should be prohibited from teaching the negroes.

Another party assembled at the missionaries' house, and destroyed their furniture, and crockery, in short, nearly all they possessed. The Governor offered the Count to obtain satisfaction for this outrage, and even promised for the future to be a father to the missionaries. But his power was not equal to his promises; for scarcely had Count Zinzendorf sailed, when a still more flagrant act of violence was committed. A party of whites, completely armed, attacked the little assembly of praying people, and the Mission House became a scene of riot and spoliation. Most of the negroes present made their escape, but one of the missionaries received a wound in his shoulder, and his wife was stabbed in the chest, while several others were severely injured. Happily for the Mission, the King of Denmark again interposed, and an order was received from the Court of Copenhagen, which put a stop to the cruel persecution they had so long experienced.

They soon after made their first visits to the adjacent islands of Santa Cruz and St. Jan.

Scarcely had the little band time to rejoice in the rest which followed on the publication of the royal rescript, when fresh trials arose. A serious visitation of cholera and yellow fever broke out, and many of the missionary brethren fell victims to these diseases.

Still the Mission grew and prospered.

Many of Mr. Martin's letters are full of interest. In one, he says, "scarcely a day passes but some of these poor creatures call upon us, bemoaning their sin and misery, and praying with floods of tears for divine grace." It appears from authentic documents, that forty, and even as many as ninety, negroes were baptized in one day.

Each succeeding year found large additions to the number of the converts, many of whom proved, by their holy and consistent lives, that old things had passed away, and that all things had become new.

So impressed were some of the owners by the change effected in their slaves, that others were induced to send from distant estates, inviting the missionaries to visit their plantations.

Much as they disliked religion themselves, many candidly confessed that the teaching which led a thievish negro to "steal no more," was good and salutary. So great was the demand for teachers, that in 1776, a party of six fresh missionaries embarked for the West Indies. They had only reached the Shetland Islands, when the vessel was wrecked; and the whole party were only too thankful to escape with their lives, having literally suffered the loss of all things. During their stay at Malsey, they were treated with the greatest hospitality, but it was not till the spring following that any vessel arrived by which they could proceed on their voyage. That vessel was bound for Norway, and our travellers showed that their hearts were indeed in their work, for no sooner had they reached that country, than finding a vessel which was bound for the West Indies, they secured a passage, and ultimately reached their destination in safety.

During the next three years, there was a fearful drought, followed by a failure of the crops.

Famine and great scarcity of water produced such distress, that numbers of the slaves were sold by their owners, and thus the Gospel was carried into distant parts.

This was followed by a contagious fever, which, in little more than a month, carried off as many as five of the missionary party.

The vessel in which they had sailed, landed them at St. Eustatius, and from thence they proceeded in an English vessel to St. Thomas's. The voyage, though short, is dangerous, on account of the numerous rocks and islets which obstruct the course. One morning, there arose a dreadful storm, which drove the vessel upon a rock, within a very short distance from the island.

The sailors at once took to the boat, but when the missionaries tried to follow, the vessel was either carried away by the waves, or they found there was no room for them. Anxious to leave the ship, they crept along the bowsprit to the rock against which she had struck. Feder, seeing a number of stones between it and the neighbouring island, resolved to attempt escaping across them to the shore. This seemed to be not only his one chance for life, but it might be the means of his extending help to his poor lame brother. With this view, he dropped down from the vessel by means of a rope, but just as he set foot on the stones, he lost his balance, was seized by the waves, and dashed among the rocks.

Beholding him rise to the surface apparently motionless, Israel gave him his parting blessing, saying,—"My dear brother, go in peace." Instantly, the body was swallowed up by the waves, and was seen no more. Poor Israel still remained upon the wreck, his lameness preventing his using any means for escape. But his mind was kept in perfect peace, contrasting, as he said, in a striking way with the storm which raged without. After a time the waves broke over the vessel, threatening it with instant destruction, and he every moment expected to be washed into the sea. But he was destined to be spared for future usefulness. Some people from the shore at length succeeded in throwing a rope to him, and he was hauled safe to land. He reached St. Thomas's, having lost the whole of his property in the wreck. So great was the change in public sentiment with regard to missionaries shortly after his arrival, that on a slave insurrection again breaking out, the Danish Governor allowed a certificate to be given to all negroes under their charge, by which they were allowed to pass the watch to and from their meetings unmolested.

CHAPTER XVIII.

ST. JAN.

> "Sow when the morning breaketh,
> In beauty o'er the land;
> And when the evening falleth,
> Withhold not thou thine hand."

LET us now take a glance, at the little West Indian Island of St. Jan.

During a visit made by that devoted missionary, Frederick Martin, to Copenhagen, he received a royal rescript, in favour of his work; and with this order he began to labour in St. Jan. Very soon after, a remarkable revival of religion took place, when from 200 to 300 slaves would flock, after their day's toil, to his evening meetings, and gladly spend their hours of rest, before retiring for the night, in the study of God's word, and in prayer. On Sundays, the congregations numbered from 800 to 900 persons, while on one day no fewer than 380 slaves gave in their names as candidates for baptism.

In the year 1749, the Moravian Bishop Watteville, made a visitation of these islands, during which he baptized and confirmed large numbers of slaves, both in St. Croix and St. Jan. He was particularly interested in one congregation, and amongst those baptized in it were several aged, blind and lame persons, who, at great personal inconvenience, had travelled some distance, to be enrolled as members of the Church.

Probably some, even of those best acquainted with the history and circumstances of the West Indies, know little of this island beyond its name. But small and insignificant as it is to the eye of man, there is doubtless in it much that is of value in the sight of God.

The Mission itself is invested with peculiar interest. The unhealthiness of the place has caused it to be called, like the Mission stations on the West Coast of Africa, the grave of Europeans.

The origin of this Mission is as follows:— Shortly after the missionaries arrived at St. Thomas in 1732, their hearts were touched by the accounts given of the state of the negroes in the sister isle.

This interest was deepened by the removal of some of their early converts to St. Jan. Anxious to know if they retained their religion, while surrounded by heathen, and deprived of all public ordinances, one of the brethren paid them a visit, and met with a hearty welcome from his children in the faith.

Soon after a good man named Jens Rasmus, who had made acquaintance with the missionaries in St. Thomas, undertook the duties of overseer in one of the plantations of St. Jan.

In those days, even Christian men had very indistinct ideas concerning the sin of slavery. Jens Rasmus seems to have been no exception to the rule. Shocked at the immorality and ignorance around him, he began to assemble all the negroes under his care, who were willing to listen, and when work was over, to speak to them about the things which pertained to their everlasting welfare. They listened, and wished to be more perfectly taught. This led the worthy overseer to write to St. Thomas, and invite Frederick Martin and the other missionaries to come over and preach to this willing people. So great was the increase of those who attended, that in 1754, fearless of the malaria which infected the air, and threatened death to any European who dared to brave it, John Bracker left his friends at St. Thomas and took up his abode amongst these sable outcasts. A small estate was purchased on which a church and mission house were built. Ere many years elapsed, this church was unfortunately blown down by one of the hurricanes which so often beset these islands. For months, this "brother beloved" and his little flock, had to hold all their services in the open air, exposed to a scorching West Indian sun. It must have been a touching sight to have seen that lonely man surrounded by his negro band, most of whom were his own spiritual children, as after the labours of the day they flocked from the plantation to join him in some quiet nook to pray to Him whom they had learned to love as their God and Father, and to receive from his hands the dying tokens of the love of Him whom they now knew as their Saviour and their Lord.

Again and again would the woods reverberate with their anthem of praise, as they sung over the much loved lines:—

> "Our love shall ne'er grow old or cold,
> Until we with Him reign."

But these converts were not satisfied with words of praise. They exhibited their devotion also by deeds of love. Stone and other materials were brought in their leisure time, and at length they had the joy of seeing a new church erected in Bethany, on the site of the old one. This accommodation not proving sufficient, another church was built, and a second missionary appointed for those who were willing to worship, but precluded by distance from joining the congregation at Bethany. And now a fresh trial awaited them. In 1793, a terrible storm swept over the island, which greatly injured both the old settlement and the new one of Emmaus. Almost all the inhabitants, white, and coloured, flocked to the old mission station, under some vague impression that there they might find safety. The hurricane still increased, till all the negro huts were swept away, and at last, the church, which was a more substantial building, fell with a tremendous crash, beams, boards, rafters and shingles, flying in all directions. The mission-house, though much injured, was not blown down. Every moment, the inmates anticipated its destruction, as it cracked and trembled to its foundation, while all within were saturated with water, which, pouring down from the roof, ran in streams through both the living and sleeping rooms. Providentially the mission house and the church at Emmaus were spared, though in a sadly delapidated state. Several hurricanes have since visited the island. That in 1819 carried away part of the roof of the mission house and church at Bethany; while at Emmaus the church suffered greatly, and every negro's house but one was washed away.

Bishop Cunon, a member of the mission board, and the Rev. T. L. Badham, one of its secretaries in England, are at the time when these pages are being written, engaged in an official visitation to the Brethren's missions in the

West Indies. Their first visit was to the Danish Islands. Mr. Badham writes from St. Jan, under date, Oct. 27th, 1862, and thus describes his visit to these very stations :—" We arranged to leave St. Thomas for St. Jan, on the 25th. A boat was to meet us at Smith-bay, opposite the west-end of St. Jan. The distance from New Herrnhutt to Smith-bay is about seven miles, and to render the journey as easy as possible, Brother Warner kindly undertook to drive us over in a small four-wheeled conveyance. The road proved to be fearfully steep, narrow, and rugged, so that our two sure-footed ponies, had difficulty in performing their task, and we could not but admire the nerve of our charioteer. We were preserved from injury, and arrived in due time on the snow-white sands of Smith-bay. Taking leave of Brother Warner, we and our luggage were carried on board the boat, we being only glad that the people did not carry us on their heads, as they do nearly everything. Our voyage was tedious, and I must acknowledge, that our admiration of the ever-varying panorama of the rocky islets, was less than if viewed from land. On the strand we were welcomed by Brother Köster, who at once accompanied us to the judge. This functionary, who is the principal official in the island, resides in the fort. One or two cannon and the

Danish flag flying serves to distinguish the building. Its situation is striking, on an almost insulated rock. Half-an-hour's ride brought us to Bethany. It is situate on a lofty, rocky knoll, bounded by deep ravines, skirted in all directions but one by loftier heights. Hill and valley are alike covered with dense bush. The church is low and small, the dwelling house is almost in the last stage of decay, chiefly through the ravages of worms. The burial ground is lower down the hill on the south. Like all in these islands, it is the resting place of members of the mission family alone, it being still the custom to bury labourers on the estates on which they have previously resided.

"It is evident that the labours of brother and sister Köster have not been in vain. He has been engaged for twenty-eight years without visiting Europe, and still preserves a marvellous amount of energy."

Sailing from St. Jan to St. Croix they landed in the pretty harbour of Christiansted. This beautiful island was sold by the Crown of France to the Danish West India Company. Count Von Pless, having bought six plantations, applied to the Brethren to send some of their number to teach his slaves. A party of fourteen volunteered to go, and, after a dangerous voyage from Copenhagen, reached the island, in 1734; but their incessant labour, added to the unhealthy climate, produced such an effect, that ten of their number died during the first year. In addition to that trial, persecution raged so fiercely, that several attempts were made to burn the houses of the missionaries and their converts. For a time they were kept in constant fear, by these repeated attempts, and the house of Ohneberg, a newly-arrived missionary, was actually burnt, though his furniture was rescued from the flames, through the aid of some faithful negroes. At one time the mission-house was occupied as a hospital for sick troops; at another time it was blown down by a hurricane. Still, amidst difficulties of every kind, this ancient mission has continued to flourish; and we will now return to Mr. Badham's letter, to learn more of its present position:—

"On a rocky knoll, overhanging the crystal waters of a little bay fringed with palms and cactuses, stands the neat, commodious school-house, with its bell in a wooden frame, on which is the inscription, 'Amstelodami, 1744,' being the first used in the mission. The church at Friedensthal possesses a nice organ, and the valley beyond is almost a grove of fruit trees, consisting of orange, tamarind, pomegranate, and other trees, overshadowing pines, arrowroot, tous-les-mois, and coffee-shrubs. In the broader portion of this lovely dell is the burial-ground, with its row of graves. How forcibly do these words call to mind the description in Holy Scripture, 'And in the garden was a sepulchre.' Adjoining is a flat spot of land, once a swamp, where stands the infant school; and the old church, which is now used as a day-school.

"On a neighbouring estate called 'Princess,' is the old House of Prayer, formerly used by the early missionaries, and near it, on a knoll in the middle of the village, is the last resting-place of that honoured servant of God, Frederick Martin. Though a good deal injured, the walls are strong, and the floor sound. A comparatively small sum would restore it, and the missionary hopes that friends at home will raise the needed funds. From Martin's grave there is a charming view of the district in which, in by-gone days, he was wont to go about, and win souls for his Saviour. As the traveller stands by his tomb, and views the eloquent relics of the past, by which he is surrounded, he is fain to exclaim, in the words of Holy Writ, 'He being dead, yet speaketh.'"

The Christian reader will delight to linger upon such pictures of primitive Christianity as are this day to be found in these far-off islands; but the limits of this little volume will only permit a reference to one more station.

This brief sketch would be incomplete without mention of Friedensfeld. It stands in a commanding position, near the centre of the island. At a short distance are the bold peaks of the Blue Mountain, and Mount Eagle. The town is surrounded by sugar-cane fields and pastures, and the station is embowered in trees and shrubs. There are numerous trees, bearing the delicious fruit called the mispel, or sappadilla. All the ravines, or water-courses, near Friedensberg, another part of this lovely island, are fringed with trees, amongst which the orange tree, with its golden burden, stands conspicuous.

The church, which is the conspicuous object for miles round, is a lofty building, with a neat cupola. The old church is now used as the Government Day-School. Between twelve and two the missionary may be seen day after day, with his dusky hearers, studying or sitting around him, regardless of heat, while he tells them of the free grace of God, and urges those who profess His faith to walk worthy of the Lord, and adorn His Gospel in all things. The church at Friedensberg is in the form of a cross. One of the most interesting estates in this neighbourhood is that called "Lower Plaisance," after Count Von Pless; the property having belonged to that early friend of the missionary, to whom reference has often been made, the Lord-Chamberlain Von

Pless. This estate was the scene of the labours of the first missionary party, and is the resting place of the ten negro brothers and sisters of whom Count Zinzendorf sang, in the prophetic spirit of confident faith, as the "Seed of the Ethiopian race."

Amongst the converts are some of peculiar interest. One is a blind man who, notwithstanding his infirmity, makes his own clothes, and is almost independent. He cheerfully views his deprivation of sight as an advantage, saying, that he never requires a candle, and can work as well by night as by day. Though deprived of natural sight, he says, he can behold "the light of the glory of God in the face of Jesus Christ."

There are eight schools in St. Croix, all under the Danish Government, and supported by grants of public money. One of the missionaries acts as general superintendent. In St. Thomas the new Dober school, called after the first honoured missionary, is proving a real blessing to the ninety negro scholars who are attending it; whilst the old Sunday-School at Nisky numbers three hundred on its books. The Honourable the Burgher Council has granted £10 a-year towards the support of the new school, and it is hoped that friends will be raised up to supply the needed funds for the maintenance of a teacher.

The children have a National Anthem, composed in these schools, and which they sing in a very spirited manner. It was delightful to hear the native teachers, with much warmth of heart, directing the little ones to the Friend of children. The committing of scripture and hymns to memory is a prominent feature in the course of instruction.

Mr. Badham tells us, that in his recent visit to these stations, he was much impressed with the earnest piety and evangelical knowledge exhibited by many of the negroes.

Upon one occasion he heard a native assistant pray, when he used this striking expression:—"Lord chastise us, if needful, with *one* hand, but draw us to Thee *with the other.*"

The people also show a general willingness to contribute out of their poverty towards the cause of the Lord, while their attachment to the ministers who labour amongst them is very great.

As a proof of the influence which these good men exercise in this island, may be mentioned a striking fact recently narrated by a naval officer, who has been cruizing in the West Indies.

Colonel Moody, who lately visited St. Jan, states that he inquired of the Governor what was the number of his garrison. The Governor replied with a smile, "Oh! our garrison is very small. We find the three missionaries quite enough."

It was from these three Danish islands that the word of life first sounded forth to the inhabitants of Jamaica, Antiqua, St. Kitt's, Barbadoes, and Tobago. So highly were the labours of the Moravians appreciated by the late King of Denmark, that, as a token of special regard, he conferred on Bönhoff, the senior missionary at St. Croix, the order of Dannebrog.

The Church of the United Brethren presents the remarkable feature of an ecclesiastical establishment having 314 missionaries in foreign lands, and about 80,000 people under their care, besides nearly 200 schools in their charge; their heathen congregations being nearly four times their own number at home.

It is impossible to read such a statement without seeing in it a commentary on the inspired words, " With God all things are possible."

CHAPTER XIX.

THE TRANSLATED BIBLE AND ITS FRIENDS.

> "Within this awful volume lies
> The mystery of mysteries;
> Happiest they of human race
> To whom their God has given grace
> To read, to fear, to hope, to pray,
> To lift the latch, and force the way;
> But better had they ne'er been born
> Than read to doubt, or read to scorn."

An account has already been given of the zeal of the Danish monarch and people in promoting Christian missions.

A passing notice of their efforts in furthering the circulation of the Bible abroad and at home, must not be omitted. It was in the year 1521, as we have already seen, that the Reformation commenced in Denmark. King Christian the Second was very anxious to have his subjects taught those doctrines which were founded upon Holy Scripture, and he made many fruitless attempts to obtain a visit from Luther himself.

After a long interval of disorder and bloodshed, Denmark, with the adjoining countries of Norway and Sweden, embraced Lutheranism, which has been the established faith ever since.

From an interesting article in "The Book and its Mission," and from the publications of the British and Foreign Bible Society, we principally gather the subjoined information about the Bible in Denmark.

There is still, in the Royal Library of Copenhagen, a very ancient manuscript of a part of the Old Testament in Danish, supposed to have been written early in the 14th century. It is strongly bound in wooden boards covered with skin, but is now fast mouldering away.

In 1515 the first attempt to present the Word of God to Denmark, in the tongue of the people, was made by Christian Pedersen, a man who was in great favour with the King, whom he accompanied in his flight into Holland. The first complete translation of the Old and New Testament was printed in 1524 by Hans Mikkelsen, the Secretary of King Christian the Second. This Danish version appeared two years before the English edition of the New Testament by Tyndale, and it is interesting to find that both translators performed part of their work at Antwerp. Copies were joyfully received in Denmark, and subsequently in Norway and Sweden, by numbers who longed for the treasure. The Bible was not, however, published as a whole, until 1550. Denmark was indebted for this boon to King Christian the Third, who engaged four or five translators, and appointed Pedersen to revise the entire work. The first edition of this entire and portable Bible consisted of 3,000 copies, and these were allotted by thousands to different parts of the kingdom. The Psalms, when first printed, were in small folio, and in a type so large that there were sometimes not more than three verses on a page.

It was about forty years after the publication of the first edition of the Bible, that Denmark, by a community of language, was privileged to introduce the sacred volume into Norway. Its introduction into that country raised up a great reformer, named, Hans Nielson Hange. This good man devoted himself to travelling through the length and breadth of the land, to make known the Book of God. In fifteen months he travelled on foot 4,000 English miles to carry the Danish Bible to his countrymen. Throughout his whole career he experienced trials of no common order. In many instances he was imprisoned. Once he was sent to the house of correction at Drontheim as a vagrant. At length his enemies succeeded, by false accusation, in obliging him to give up his work; and they conveyed him, loaded with chains, as a criminal to Christiania. He was sentenced both to fine and imprisonment; his incarceration extended over ten long years. Professor Stenierson says of him, "Scarcely any layman has appeared since the days of Peter Waldo, who with greater earnestness has sought to keep to the written word of God."

Early in the 17th century fresh efforts for the extension of that Word in Denmark were made under the auspices of the greatest monarch the country ever had, King Frederick the Fourth. Even when young, his biographer tells us, it was his habit to read many chapters of the Bible regularly morning and evening. The subsequent acts of his life proved the beneficial influence of that early habit. Much of the value for the Word of God, which has existed even at the worst times in Denmark, must doubtless be traced to the influence of that noble prince.

In modern times, the efforts of that most wonderful of modern institutions, the British and Foreign Bible Society, have greatly fostered the reverence for the Bible in Denmark. Foremost amongst those, who in later days contributed to the dissemination of the Bible in Denmark, was Dr. Henderson. In early life he offered himself to a Scotch Society to be sent as a missionary to India. Like his predecessors in the work, he found that the British possessions in that country were unapproachable by a Christian missionary in a British vessel. A short time before the Messrs. Haldane had sought permission from the Directors of the East India Company to take out a band of labourers to that land, when they met with a positive refusal. The only access for a missionary was by a Danish vessel: and so in 1805 we find Henderson and Patterson, like another Ziegenbalg and Plutscho, at Copenhagen, whence they hoped to secure a passage to the East.

But God had other work for his servants to do. Whilst detained in that city they began to labour actively for their Master. They distributed Danish Bibles, and were warmly aided in their undertaking by men of all ranks in that country. A Copenhagan paper stated, that "they were men of irreproachable character, and preached with great applause."

Miss Henderson's Memoir of her excellent father contains much that is deeply interesting. Each day convinced the strangers that there was a great work to do in Denmark as well as in India; and while making every effort to secure a passage to that land, they wrote to Scotland earnestly requesting, that some one might be sent to carry on the work they had begun at Copenhagen and Elsinore. Pending the answer, they heard of a vessel that was to sail to the East. Dr. Henderson hastened to secure berths, but on reaching the office not one was to be obtained. He offered to go in the steerage, or even to sleep on deck; but the steerage was full, and the latter alternative was positively refused. Thus obliged to remain in Denmark, they heartily entered upon the wide field of usefulness so unexpectedly opened before them. Meantime, a letter from Scotland arrived, stating that the small Society could only support two labourers; and as the way to India seemed for the present closed, it would sustain them in the interval in Denmark. Dr. Henderson at once took steps to promote a more general diffusion of the Word of God. Amongst many kind friends raised up to render him aid, were Dr. Thorkelin, Knight of the Dannebrog, and the Rev. Dr. Münter, Bishop of Zealand. Through the influence of that prelate the first Bible Society meeting was held in the Episcopal Palace, when Chevalier Peter Bröndsted, Privy Counsellor of Legation to his late Majesty, and several learned Danish professors, were present. Dr. Henderson joyfully speaks of that day as the one on which Denmark's life-boat was launched. Amongst the first to enter his name as a supporter of the Society was the venerable Landgrave Charles of Hesse-Cassel, grandson of George the Second of England. He accepted the office of president, and with his Royal Consort, Louisa, daughter of King Frederick the Fifth of Denmark, evinced unabated attachment to the cause of the Bible Society till his death. His anniversary speeches were remarkable, being in fact specimens of a royal sermon, as his invariable custom was to select a text on which he founded a short, but most appropriate discourse. One year he took Amos viii. 11; from this text he commented upon Denmark's temporal mercies and spiritual destitution. Another year he gave the history of the Law as lost in the days of Manasseh and Amos, and found and declared by the High Priest Hilkiah.

The twofold connection of Prince Charles with the reigning family made his patronage extremely valuable. It is an interesting fact, that one of the first members of the Bible Society Committee at Copenhagen was a brother of the Danish Mrs. Carey, of Serampore, and himself brought to know and value that Book through the instrumentality of the Serampore missionary and his wife. Another valued assistant was the kind-hearted and zealous Mr. Van der Smissen, one of the converts of the Rev. George Whitfield. The seed sown in India and England was bearing fruit in Denmark.

As in the days of the Apostles, so it has been ever since. In all countries God has raised up honourable women, not a few, to aid in making known His word of truth. Denmark was no exception to this rule. Amongst the early champions for God's Word there were many of the female members of the royal House of Denmark.

In addition to the Princess Louisa of Hesse, of whom mention has already been made, the Princess Christian, daughter of the Duke of Holstein Sonderburg Augustenburg, who afterwards graced the throne of Denmark on her royal husband's accession as Christian VIII., took a lively interest in the good work. She had herself read Buchanan's Researches and other missionary works, in German, and she afforded to the Bible and Mission cause all the aid of her exalted position.

The widowed Duchess of Augustenburg, only daughter of King Christian VII., openly expressed her interest in this work. The Countesses Stolberg and Reventlow are gratefully mentioned by Dr. Henderson as showing much concern for the spread of Gospel truths. The death of the last named lady was a severe loss to all connected with the cause of Christ in Denmark. In an account of her, published in 1816, we find this statement: "We have great reason to deplore the loss of a noble patroness, the Countess Julia of Reventlow, who has terminated a life full of suffering, but wholly dedicated to the promulgation of Christianity. Even from her sick bed, she promoted the diffusion of the Holy Scriptures to such a degree, that she has erected a lasting monument to herself in the hearts of all who are friends to the Divine Word."

The impression left on the mind by the perusal of Dr. Henderson's Memoirs, as to the willingness of the Danish people to avail themselves of efforts made for their spiritual benefit, is fully borne out by Dr. Patterson's statements in his "Book for every Land." He gives an interesting account of his early attempts to acquire the language, and his subsequent success in translations, and after publishing the tract, called "The one thing needful," he says: "Our chief occupation now consisted in the distribution of these tracts, which we did publicly as in England. We went to the Royal Gardens, where we gave a tract to every person we met. We took long walks in the country, and met multitudes on the roads, returning from the market in town, to whom we never failed to give one of these little messengers of mercy. Those to whom we offered them often drew back their hand when a tract was presented, but on our saying, in half-English, half-Danish, 'It costs nothing,' 'Coster naething,' they smiled, saying 'So, so,' and took it."

In conclusion, we cannot do better than quote from the Annual Report of the British and Foreign Bible Society, for 1863, which contains the following statements: "New ties bind England to Denmark.

The auspicious alliance, which has so closely united the Royal Families of the two countries, will deepen the interest of all British Christians in the spiritual welfare of Denmark.

"The agency for the dissemination of the Sacred Scriptures in the kingdom of Denmark have prosecuted their operations without interruption during the twelve months extending from the 1st February, 1862, to the 31st January, 1863. In that period the issues from the Agency's Depôt have comprised a total of 16,136 copies of the Sacred Scriptures, consisting of New Testaments in three separate editions, and copies of the Book of Psalms. Although the number of copies issued during the preceding year—namely, 11,396—might in view of our position and circumstances have been regarded as a very large issue, it will be seen that that number has, to our great gratification, been exceeded to a considerable extent. Since we began our actual operations in the second half of the year 1856, we have been enabled to put into circulation not fewer than 58,545 copies of the Scriptures.

"As in former years, a number of clergymen, and an increasing number of schoolmasters, have applied to us for copies of the Scriptures. The largest demands for copies have reached us from Bornholm, an island in the Baltic. Some few

Bible Societies and Bible Associations have also applied to us. Among the individual applicants for supplies of the Scriptures, who have addressed themselves to the Agency, may be mentioned Her Majesty the Queen Dowager, for her school for poor girls; the Poor Commission connected with the Corporation of Copenhagen; and the authorities of the House of Correction in Viborg.

"The Colportage work, commenced in the year 1861, has been continued and extended. The whole of the city and the suburbs, the crews on board the vessels in the harbour, and the inhabitants of the poorer districts of the city, have been visited by the Colporteurs; and they have likewise extended their operations to the neighbouring towns and the country villages. By this means not less than 5,391 copies of the Scriptures have been brought into the hands of our population.

"The Bible Agent says, 'As the Committee of the Society requested me, during my visit to London, to endeavour to do something towards supplying the men in the Danish army with copies of the Scriptures, I availed myself of the opportunity afforded by a large number of troops being collected together last autumn for drill and exercise, to send a Colporteur amongst them, who succeeded in selling 600 copies of the New Testament.'

"An Association formed here, with the designation, 'Church Association for Home Missions,' commenced, towards the close of last year, very extended efforts for the dissemination of the sacred Scriptures, and to meet their requirements they ordered from the Agency not less than 839 copies. In connexion with this Association there are Mission Stations in various localities in Zealand, in Fühnen, and on the eastern side of Jutland, all of which present channels for the diffusion of the Scriptures.

"It may be added, that in many places in the country, the clergy have small Depôts of the Scriptures, whence they supply the people residing in their respective neighbourhoods."

The Bible is also largely circulated in Iceland. That more do not have recourse to the Agency, is doubtless owing to the circumstance that there are now so many Auxiliaries to the Danish Bible Society in operation throughout the country; and it may likewise be attributed to the fact, that many persons do not care to order New Testaments without the references.

It is gratifying to find that the importance of reverence for the word of God, is thus recognised by one of the Dignitaries of the Danish Church. The Bishop of Adensee, writes thus in reference to the spread of the Bible in that country. "With regard to the christian tendency of the coming time, a great deal will depend, on whether children, from ten to fourteen years of age, are made acquainted with the Word of God; for what they learn in youth, they will not forget in old age; and when life brings sorrows and troubles, they will *then* know, where to turn for consolation and blessing."

Having thus glanced at Bible work in Denmark, let us see what it has done abroad.

We have seen in an earlier chapter, that Ziegenbalg and Plutscho, the first Danish missionaries, on the Coromandel coast, were the instruments chosen by God, to commence the great work of translating the Holy Scriptures into the languages of the East.

We have followed those lonely men in imagination, as they spelt out letter by letter; and wrote their first words and sentences, with an iron pen, upon the leaf of the palmyra tree. Their own accounts have told us of the prayers and tears which accompanied their work, and of the delight and thanksgiving with which after months of toil, they realised the joyful fact, that *one chapter* of the Word of Life, was actually translated into an Eastern tongue.

In laying down the report from which we have just quoted, and comparing the past with the present, the Christian reader is fain to exclaim, "Behold how great a matter a little fire kindleth."

The Bible is now translated either in whole or in part, into no less than eighty-five eastern languages or dialects.

It was not till 1818, that an Indian branch of the Bible Society was established.

A report published in Calcutta, contains the details of the formation of that Indian branch.

We find that it was after a sermon preached by the sainted Henry Martyn, that a few Christian gentlemen, foremost amongst whom was the Rev. David Brown, formed themselves into the Calcutta Auxilliary, in connection with that Society.

From that period the Bible began to make its way into more distant parts of the Indian Empire; and soon the results began to appear.

The writer is aware, that the objection is often urged by those who themselves neglect the Holy Volume, that such translations involve much needless expense, and that the natives themselves are indifferent to their circulation.

That the majority abroad, as well as at home, are culpably indifferent to the Book of God, is a lamentable fact. But that in many cases, the natives are thirsting for it, is happily a well established fact.

Out of the mass of evidence which might be

adduced in proof of this assertion the writer would cite the following interesting cases.

The news of the formation of the Calcutta branch of the Bible Society, soon spread to distant parts of India, and touching were the appeals which came from natives in various quarters, entreating that they too might be blessed with copies of the Word of God. One convert writes thus:—" Through the paternal compassion of the Rev. Mr. Kolhoff, I am placed in the vineyard, which the living God has planted in this country; but can a vine, without pouring water upon it, grow in a flourishing way, so as to give ripened fruits? It is impossible. Therefore, your petitioner thirsteth very much for the spiritual waters of the Holy Bible, so needful for salvation."

In a village near Dacca, a number of natives were found by a missionary, who were described as very remarkable for their moral lives, and love of truth. Anxious to know to what Hindoo sect they belonged, he was told by their leader, that they were in search of the true gooroo or teacher. When asked where they had heard of him, the answer was, in a book. At length one of their number carefully unfolded a parcel, and from it, drew a book, part of the New Testament, much worn; *kept in a case of brass, which had been made for the purpose of preserving it, and which they said had been there for many years,* though none of them knew from whence it came.

Three of their number were soon after baptized. Many years ago, a gentleman going through a village near Calcutta, left a Bengal New Testament in a native shop. Within a year, three or four of the most intelligent inhabitants came to Serampore, to find out more about this wonderful book. Soon six persons abjured Hindooism and were baptized. Amongst these, was an old man, named Juggernauth, who had long been a devotee to that idol in Orissa, and had acquired a great name for sanctity. On his first reading the New Testament, he hung the image of Krishnoo, which he had for years worshipped, on a tree in his garden, and ultimately cleft it up to boil his rice. He continued for many years to adorn the Christian faith, and to explain the Scriptures to all who resorted to him.

CONCLUSION.

"HE MUST REIGN."

> "Come, Lord, and wipe away
> The curse, the sin, the stain,
> And make this blighted world of ours
> Thine own fair world again.
> Come, then, Lord Jesus, come!"—BONAR.

WE must now take leave of Denmark and her noble band of missionary labourers.

The writer is fully conscious of the imperfections of this volume. Where so much might be truthfully said, it has, indeed, been no easy task to select and abridge. But if the impression left on the mind of the reader be at all similar to that entertained by the writer, we shall not part from our Danish brethren without a feeling of regret.

Of the labours and self-denial of these devoted men, it may truly be said, "The half has not been told."

In the details of this work, it has been the desire to understate, rather than overstate, every fact. It is, however, impossible for any candid mind to read such an unvarnished statement without being compelled to come to the conclusion of the Apostle, that, "the Gospel is the power of God unto salvation;" and that this is the case alike with the polished nations of the East, the rude untutored Greenlanders, and the poor benighted slaves of the West Indies.

It is, in truth, the only effectual instrument of blessing, both to the souls and bodies of men.

In the Inspired Volume we are told, "that in the mouth of two or three witnesses shall every word be established."

In conclusion, therefore, from amongst a host of such witnesses, the testimony of two,—both impartial and independent—will be selected.

The evidence of the first will prove the value of the missionaries, as mere agents of civilization amongst the most barbarous tribes of South Africa. The testimony of the second speaks of their moral and religious influence amongst the warlike and ferocious inhabitants of British Columbia.

Neither of the authors quoted is connected with the work of Missions, or pre-possessed in favour of the workers.

The first witness is the African hunter and traveller, Mr. Baldwin, whose book is addressed mainly to sporting men.

He states that his wanderings brought him into frequent contact with missionaries; and he thus simply tells how their work struck him, as a hunter and a man of the world. Writing of the German missionaries at Natal, he says, "They are all six active energetic fellows and good workmen, and have, in the space of six weeks, built themselves a good substantial house, with a wide verandah on three sides. They are clever, learned, well-informed men, and pass every spare moment in hard study in acquiring the Bechuana language, which is no easy matter, as they have only the New Testament, translated by Moffatt, to assist them. They are happy, hospitable fellows and make most excellent colonists, being able to turn their hands to anything in the world!"

The second witness shall be Commander Mayne, R.N., author of "Four Years in British Columbia, and Vancouver's Island." It is very remarkable that Mr. Duncan, to whom he refers, left England, in Dec., 1856, at the request of another British officer, Captain Prevost, R.N., to commence a mission amongst the Tsimshean Indians, in the neighbourhood of the Rocky Mountains. The gallant captain kindly offered a free passage to a missionary, if the Church Missionary Society would send one. Mr. Duncan reached Vancouver's Island, in June, 1857. Commander Mayne, referring to him, says :—

"There is no doubt that men of Mr. Duncan's stamp who will in a frank, manly spirit go among the heathen, diffusing the blessings of religion and education, will meet with a cordial reception, and an abundant reward."

He mentions that Captain Richards stated in his despatch that he had had some trouble with the Indians, and, at a large meeting, they had asked him why Mr. Duncan was not sent to teach them, instead of the Tsimshean Indians. In conversation, Captain Richards said, that the business he had just had with the Indians convinced him that it was not *our ships of war* that were wanted up the coast, but *missionaries*. That officer says:—

"The Indian's ignorance of *our* power, and strong confidence in *his own*, in addition to his natural savage temper, renders him unfit to be dealt with at present by stern and unyielding men of war, unless his destruction be contemplated, which, of course, it is not." Captain Richards adds, "Why do not more men come out, since your mission has been so successful; or, if the Missionary Societies cannot afford them, why does not Government send out fifty men, and place them up the coast at once? Surely it would not be difficult to find fifty good men in England, willing to engage in such a work. And their expenses would be almost nothing compared with the cost, which the country must sustain to subdue the Indians by force of arms." "Such" writes Commander Mayne, "are the earnest sentiments of one of her Majesty's Naval Captains, while among the Indians. And such, I may add, are the sentiments of myself, in common, I believe, with all my brother officers—after nearly *five years'* constant and close intercourse with the natives of Vancouver's Island, and the coast of British Columbia."*

In another chapter, Commander Mayne says, "Mr. Duncan's name always acts as a talisman." Again and again, this English officer had the question put to him by the Indians, "Why was no one sent to teach them what was right? Why was not a missionary sent to show them better ways?" Even these heathen cannibals quarrelled amongst themselves as to who should have the honour of Mr. Duncan's presence in their respective districts.

For the details of Mr. Duncan's labours, our readers must be referred to the work just quoted, and to the publications of the Church Missionary Society. Already a spirit of inquiry is aroused. One man told Mr. Duncan, that "he and his people did not know about God, but they wanted to know, and to learn to be good." Another refused, when ill, to see the medicine-man. Mr. Duncan says, "This is the first instance in which I have known the power of their medicine-men, or women, to be slighted. Amongst all these tribes, the influence

* Maynes's "British Columbia," p. 212.

of the medicine-man, as a means of spiritual tyranny and of civil oppression, has been irresistible until broken down by Christianity." One chief told him that he and his people are stedfast in their purpose to end that abominable system. Another chief opened his house as a school, and a hundred and fifty boys were attending it. His congregations now sometimes number 200 persons. On one occasion when setting the great truths of the Gospel before them, (which he is now able to do in the Tsimshean language) one man exclaimed, several times, 'Good news! Good news!' Another said, 'It is true,' which is equivalent in their way of speaking to 'I believe.' Commander Mayne adds, "They all seemed thankful for my visit, and fully believed it would not be long before the Indians would be altogether changed. Before 1857, no Protestant missionary had ever traversed the wilds of British Columbia, nor had any attempt been made to instruct the Indians. I must except the exertions of the Roman Catholic priests."

Commander Mayne here makes a statement to which every reader is requested to pay careful attention. It so remarkably accords with the sentiments expressed by the Early Danish Missionaries on the Coromandel coast, that, if dates and places were changed, the opinion might be regarded as identical. It is almost impossible for any enlightened mind to peruse the following simple statement, and not come to the conclusion that Romanism in 1710, and Romanism in 1857 and in 1863, are identical: and that, as it was not then, so it is not now, calculated to confer any benefit either on the polished heathen of Tranquebar, or the cannibal savage of British Columbia.

Mr. Mayne thus proceeds:—

"If the opinion of the Hudson Bay people in the interior is to be relied upon, the Roman Catholic priests effected no real change in the condition of the natives. The sole result of their residence among them was, that the Indians who had been brought under their influence had imbibed some notions of the Deity, almost as vague as their own traditions. Occasionally, too, might be seen in their lodges pictures purporting to represent the roads to heaven and hell, in which there was no single suggestion of the danger of vice and crime, but a great deal of the peril of Protestantism. These coloured prints gave a pictorial history of the human race, from the time when Adam and Eve wandered in the garden down to the Reformation. Here, the one road was split into two. By one way, the Roman Catholic portion of the world were seen trooping to bliss, the other ended in a steep, bottomless precipice, over which Protestants might be seen falling. Upon the more sensible Indians, teaching such as this had little effect. Its influence was illustrated, in 1857, at Victoria, where a Roman Catholic bishop and priests had resided for some time. A cross was erected in the village, and some of them had been baptized; but when these were called before the bishop for confirmation, they refused to come unless more blankets were given them, than had been given at their baptism."

Such indirect testimonies to the usefulness of Protestant missions are, thank God, not uncommon in these days. The "Church Missionary Record" for September, 1863, contains a very interesting letter from Mr. Duncan, and an extract of a letter from Mr. Cunningham, who has recently joined him. It appears from them, that Mr. Duncan has commenced a new Mission Village about fifteen or twenty miles from Fort Simpson. Above one-fourth of the Tsimsheans from Fort Simpson, a few from Tongass, Nishkah, Keethrahtle, and Keetsahlass Indians, which tribes occupy a circle about seventy miles from Fort Simpson, have been there gathered out from the heathen through much labour and persecution. From 400 to 600 attend Divine Service on Sundays. About 100 children attend the day, and

100 adults the evening, school. The Governor of Vancouver's Island and British Columbia has marked his approval of the mission by kindly giving £50 towards the settlement of the Indians in their new colony. The Bishop of Columbia recently baptized seventy of these Indians.

The same number of the "Church Missionary Record" contains also a remarkable testimony to the result of missionary work amongst the Karens, communicated to the "Friend of India" newspaper, by Colonel Phayre, Commissioner of British Burmah.

It is, however, needless to refer to this at length. In the presence of tens of thousands of converts from Tinnevelly and other parts of India; multitudes in the South Sea Islands, from China, from America, and from Africa, changed by the power of the Gospel into devout and orderly Christians; and of the accumulated testimony of travellers, officers in the army and navy, civilians, governors, and, in fact, men of all classes, it is impossible to doubt that the Gospel is the great, and the only, agent ordained by our blessed Lord to remedy the spiritual and temporal ills of our fallen world. Dark as is the moral and religious condition of the heathen world, there are, as we have just seen, some lighter shades which the Christian will contemplate with pleasure. Some rays of truth have penetrated the gloom ; and while a darkness, like that in Egypt of old, rests upon a vast portion of the habitable world, here and there a Goshen may be found where they have "light in their dwellings."

Had the Saviour's parting injunction, "Go ye into all the world and preach the Gospel to every creature," been faithfully obeyed by His Church, in what a different condition would the world now have been! Never, since the time of our Lord's death, have there been such opportunities as now exist for fulfilling this divine command. There is scarcely a portion of the globe where Christ may not now be openly preached, and from tribe after tribe there are constant and urgent appeals for Christian missions. Shall these appeals be in vain? Shall we, Protestant Christians, permit our brothers, for whom Christ died, to perish for lack of knowledge? "How shall they believe in Him of whom they have not heard? And how shall they hear without a preacher? *And how shall they preach, except they be sent?*" Rom. x. 14, 15.

In conclusion, we would quote the words of the beloved and ever-to-be-lamented Prince Consort at the third Jubilee of the Incorporated Society for the Propagation of the Gospel in Foreign Parts, in 1851 :—

"We are thankfully acknowledging the Divine favour which has attended exertions during the lapse of 150 years. We invoke the further continuance of that favour, pledging ourselves not to relax in our efforts to extend to those of our brethren who are settled in distant lands, those blessings of Christianity which form the foundation of our community, and of our State. This, the third jubilee, falls in a happy epoch, when peace is established in Europe, and religious fervor is rekindled, and at an auspicious moment, when we are celebrating a festival of the civilization of mankind, to which all quarters of the globe have contributed their productions, and are sending their people, for the first time recognizing their advancement as a common good, their interests as identical, their mission on earth the same. And this civilization *rests on Christianity, could only be raised* on Christianity, *can only be maintained by Christianity!* I have no fear for her (the Church's) safety and ultimate welfare *so long* as she holds fast to what our ancestors gained for us at the Reformation—*the Gospel and the unfettered right of its use.*"

Works for the Young,

PUBLISHED BY

MESSRS. SEELEY, JACKSON, & HALLIDAY,

54 FLEET STREET.

A Child's Warfare; or, the Conquest of Self. By MADELINE E. HEWER. Second Edition. With Frontispiece. Small 8vo. cloth, 3s. 6d.

Agathos, and other Sunday Stories. By the BISHOP OF OXFORD. Engravings, 18mo. 2s. 6d., cloth.

Aids to Development. Fourth Edition. Foolscap 8vo. cloth, 6s.

A Manual for the Young. An Exposition of Proverbs I.-IX. By the Rev. CHARLES BRIDGES, M.A. In royal 18mo. cloth, 2s. 6d.

Anna; or, Passages from the Life of a Daughter at Home. Sixth Edition. Foolscap 8vo. cloth, 3s. 6d.

Baillie (Rev. John) Rivers in the Desert; or, Mission Scenes in Burmah. With Engravings. Fourth Thousand. Small 8vo. cloth, 5s.

—— **Life Studies; or, How to Live.** With Engravings. Small 8vo. cloth, 5s.

BROCK (Mrs. Carey)

—— **Margaret's Secret and its Success.** Crown 8vo. Frontispiece, 5s.

—— **The Rectory and the Manor. A Tale.** Fourth Thousand. With Frontispiece, cloth, 5s.

—— **Sunday Echoes in Week-Day Hours.** With a Preface by the Lord Bishop of Winchester. Third Thousand. 5s.

—— **Children at Home. A Tale from Real Life.** Eighth Thousand. With Engraving, cloth, 5s.

—— **Working and Waiting. A Tale.** The Fifth Thousand. With Engraving, cloth, 5s.

—— **Home Memories; or, Echoes of a Mother's Voice.** Fifth Thousand. With Engraving, cloth, 5s.

—— **Almost Persuaded. A Tale of Village Life.** Fourth Thousand. With Frontispiece, cloth, 1s. 6d.

—— **The Little Missionary; or, More Ways than One.** With Engraving, 18mo. cloth, 6d.

—— **Making the Best of It.** With Engraving. 18mo. cloth, 6d.

First Steps in Life: Tales for the Young.
By Mrs. GELDART, Author of "Strength in Weakness." Second Edition. Coloured Frontispiece. 5s.

Fresh Gatherings for Christian Children.
With Engravings. 18mo. cloth, 2s. 6d.

Lamp of Life (The). A Grandmother's Story. With Engravings. 18mo. cloth, 1s.

Land of Promise (The). An Account of the Chosen People and the Holy Land. By Mrs. BARKER. With Frontispiece. Small 8vo. cloth, 3s. 6d.

Litton (Rev. E. A., M.A.). Guide to the Study of Holy Scripture. With Maps. Small 8vo. cloth, 5s.

Mackenzie (Rev. W. B.) The Wanderer and his Return Home. Thoughts for Young Men. Small 8vo. cloth, 1s. 6d.

—— The Lamp to the Path, with a Calen-dar for Reading the Scriptures through in a Year. Fifth Edition. 18mo. cloth, 1s.

Many Crowns; the Names and Titles of the Lord Jesus. With a Preface by the Rev. CANON CHAMPNEYS. Third Thousand. 32mo. cloth limp, 1s. 6d.

Margaret Warner; or, the Young Wife at the Farm. By the Author of "Nursery Influence." Second Edition. With Frontispiece. Small 8vo. cloth, 3s. 6d.

Martyn (Rev. H.) Life and Letters. By the Rev. JOHN SARGENT, M.A. With a Portrait. A New and Revised Edition. Small 8vo. cloth, 5s.

Mayo (Miss) Lessons on Objects. Seventeenth Edition. Foolscap 8vo. boards, 3s. 6d.

— Lessons on Shells. Second Edition. Foolscap 8vo. with Ten Plates, cloth, 3s. 6d.

— Lessons on the Miracles of our Blessed Lord. Foolscap 8vo. cloth, 3s. 6d.

M'Gregor (J. Esq.) Three Days in the East. Engravings. Second Edition. 18mo. boards, 1s.

Memorials of Two Sisters. Fifth Edition. Foolscap 8vo. cloth, 4s. 6d.

Message of Life. Second Edition. Fcap. 8vo. cloth, 2s. 6d.

Monod (Rev. A.) God is Love. An Exposition of 1 John, iv. 8. Foolscap 8vo. cloth, 1s. 6d.

Montmorency. A Roman Catholic Tale. Foolscap 8vo. cloth, 4s. 6d.

More (Hannah) Life of, with Selections from her Correspondence. Edited by the LORD BISHOP OF RIPON. With a Portrait. Price 1s. 6d. in limp cloth, or 2s. in cloth, red edges.

Newton (Rev. John) Life of, with Selec-
tions from his Correspondence. Edited by the LORD BISHOP
OF RIPON. With a Portrait. Price 1s. 6d. in limp cloth, or
2s. in cloth, red edges.

Osburn's (William) Israel in Egypt, or the
Books of Genesis and Exodus illustrated by Existing Monuments. Second Edition. In crown 8vo. with numerous
wood engravings, 5s. cloth.

Our Native Land; a History of England
for the Young. By the Author of "Scriptural Instruction for
the Least and Lowest." 2 vols. 18mo. cloth, 6s.

Perils among the Heathen: Incidents in
Missionary Life. With Preface by the Rev. J. RIDGEWAY, M.A.
Six Engravings. 5s.

Pitcairn (Rev. D.) Bud of Promise. Me-
moir of ELIZA H. M. GRÆME. With Portrait. Third Thousand. Foolscap 8vo. cloth, 3s. 6d.

Puddicombe (Julia) Little Mary Grown
Older. 18mo. cloth, 2s.

Reward-Books for the Young. By a
Clergyman's Wife. In Two Packets, 1s. each.

Richmond (Rev. L.) Domestic Portraiture;
being Memoirs of Three of his Children. With Engravings.
Eighth Edition. Foolscap 8vo. cloth, 5s.

School and Home; or, Leaves from a Boy's Journal. By the Author of "England's Daybreak." Crown 8vo. Frontispiece. 5s. cloth.

Scriptural Instruction for the Least and Lowest. Fifth Edition. 3 vols. 18mo. cloth, 7s. 6d.

— **The New Testament Volume,** sold separately, cloth, 2s. 6d.

Selections of Poetry for Reading and Study. In crown 8vo. With a Frontispiece and Vignette Title. Cloth, 6s.

Sermons to Young People. By Rev. M. M. PRESTON. Second Edition, 8vo. cloth, 5s.

Stevenson (Rev. John, D.D.) Perfect Love. Memorials of John and Elizabeth Wolfe. Second Edition. Foolscap 8vo. cloth, 2s. 6d.

Strength in Weakness. Memoir of WILLIAM GELDART. By Mrs. GELDART. Third Edition. With Portrait. Cloth, 3s. 6d.

The Adopted Child: a Story Illustrative of the Spirit of Adoption. By the Author of "Katherine Douglas." With Frontispiece. Small 8vo. cloth, 3s. 6d.

The Children of Long Ago. By the Author of "Words for Women." In Royal 16mo. with Twelve Engravings, cloth, 2s. 6d.

The White House at St. Real; a Tale for Schoolboys. Translated from the French of Madame E. de Pressensé. Frontispiece. 5s.

Waters from the Sanctuary: Stories suggested by the Church Services. In 18mo. Price 2s. 6d. cloth.

Whately (Miss M. L.) Ragged Life in Egypt. Third Edition. Six Engravings. 3s. 6d.

—— More about Ragged Life in Egypt. Small 8vo. Six Engravings. 3s. 6d.

Words for the Little Ones; or, Simple Lessons on Gospel Truths. By the Author of "Scriptural Instruction for the Least and Lowest." 16mo. cloth, 2s.

Work for All: and other Tales. By C. E. B. In 16mo. With Three Engravings. Cloth, 2s. 6d.

SEELEY, JACKSON, AND HALLIDAY,

54 FLEET STREET, LONDON.

LONDON:
STRANGEWAYS AND WALDEN, PRINTERS,
28 Castle St. Leicester Sq.

www.ingramcontent.com/pod-product-compliance
Lightning Source LLC
Chambersburg PA
CBHW032115230426
43672CB00009B/1739